ITEM

D0411972

UXBRIDGE COLLEGE LEARNING CENTRE
Park Road, Uxbridge, Middlesex UB8 1NQ
Telephone: 01895 853326/8

Please return this item to the Learning Centre on
or before the last date stamped below:

UXBRIDGE
UC
COLLEGE

04. 94

10. 06. ??

13. 04. 99

PAULIN T.   808·818
Faber Book of Vernacular Verse

UXBRIDGE COLLEGE LIBRARY

The Faber Book of Vernacular Verse

by the same author

A State of Justice
The Strange Museum
Liberty Tree
The Riot Act: A version of Sophocles' *Antigone*
The Faber Book of Political Verse (ed.)
The Hillsborough Script: A Dramatic Satire
Fivemiletown
Seize the Fire: A version of Aeschylus's *Prometheus Bound*
Thomas Hardy: The Poetry of Perception (Macmillan)
Ireland and the English Crisis (Bloodaxe)

The Faber Book of
VERNACULAR VERSE

Edited by TOM PAULIN

faber and faber
LONDON · BOSTON

First published in 1990
by Faber and Faber Limited
3 Queen Square London WC1N 3AU

Photoset by Wilmaset Birkenhead Wirral
Printed in England by
Clays Ltd St Ives plc Bungay Suffolk

All rights reserved

This collection © Tom Paulin 1990

A CIP record for this book is
available from the British Library.

ISBN 0-571-14470-5

Contents

Editor's Note

For their help and assistance, I'm deeply grateful to Jonathan Barker, Mary Enright and the staff of the Arts Council of Great Britain Poetry Library, Margaret Berry, Angus Calder, Robert Cockroft, Tony Crowley, Brian Friel, David Hammond, Seamus Heaney, Brian Hollingworth, Jasvinder Khosa, John Lanchester, Blake Morrison, Bernard and Heather O'Donoghue, George Parfitt, Thorlac Turville-Petre, David Young and the staff of the Nottingham University Library. My own wains, Michael and Niall, have also taught me a lot about the joy and energy of oral tradition, its stars of wonder, stars of bright.

Introduction

Some time back in the solid quiet of the 1950s, at primary school in Belfast, I came across this passage from *Huckleberry Finn* framed by the black official rubric of a comprehension exercise:

I made two mile and a half, and then struck out a quarter of a mile or more towards the middle of the river, because pretty soon I would be passing the ferry landing and people might see me and hail me. I got out amongst the drift-wood and then laid down in the bottom of the canoe and let her float. I laid there and had a good rest and a smoke out of my pipe, looking away into the sky, not a cloud in it. The sky looks ever so deep when you lay down on your back in the moonshine; I never knowed it before. And how far a body can hear on the water such nights! I heard people talking at the ferry landing. I heard what they said, too, every word of it. One man said it was getting towards the long days and the short nights, now. 'Tother one said *this* warn't one of the short ones, he reckoned – and then they laughed, and he said it over again and they laughed again; then they waked up another fellow and told him, and laughed, but he didn't laugh; he ripped out something brisk and said let him alone. The first fellow said he 'lowed to tell it to his old woman – she would think it was pretty good; but he said that warn't nothing to some things he had said in his time. I heard one man say it was nearly three o'clock, and he hoped daylight wouldn't wait more than about week longer.

Huck's limber prose is a spoken prose, carefully worked to make it sound as natural and informal as the impromptu conversation he hears and reports. This is speech within speech, forming in a child's canny observant wonder, and on that first reading those voices crossing the still Mississippi in a resonant darkness had much more than a pointless banality. Like one of Wordsworth's time-spots, the prose has a visionary actuality I still can't fathom.

Many years later, I came across the last verse of St John's Gospel:

And there are also many other things which Jesus did, the which, if they should be written every one, I suppose that even the world itself could not contain the books that should be written.

The relaxed wonder and spontaneous innocence of that sentence come out from under the more formal rhetoric of the previous verses so that we seem to hear the voice of the translator, fresh and almost child-like now that the public statement has been made. Like Twain's prose, the biblical verse has a vernacular authenticity that bonds the reader in an immediate, personal manner.

Perhaps it's the official *gravitas* of public discourse, its chilling lack of kinship ties, that is the real target in

> Latin is a dead tongue
> dead as dead can be

Many vernacular poets might want to join in that kids' chant. Latin belongs to institutions, committees, public voices, print. Against that Parnassian official order, the springy, irreverent, chanting, quartzy, often tender and intimate, vernacular voice speaks for an alternative community that is mostly powerless and invisible. This oral community voices itself in a gestural tactile language – 'freedom a come oh!' – which printed texts with their editorial apparatus of punctuation and authoritative capitals can often deaden.

Reading these lines

> You shall have a fishy
> in a little dishy
> you shall have a fishy
> when the boät comes in

we need to hear 'boät' not as *bot*, but as the Northumbrian bisyllabic *bo-uht*. Often the editorial standardization of spelling flattens out vocal difference, and the same is true of the omission of the umlaut in Hopkins's 'black hoürs' where the two crucial dots foreground the Ulster-Elizabethan accent to create a dark, resonant pentameter line. That heavy guttural 'howers' appears in the singular in Faustus's final soliloquy, and at least to my ear has a much more interesting vocal tone than the standard, monosyllabic, very lightweight pronunciation *owrs* which has largely replaced it.

Such savoured cadences put us in touch with the passionate variety of regional speech, a speech whose often sensuous sound-patterns Whitman celebrates:

The smoke of my own breath,
Echoes, ripples, buzz'd whispers, love-root, silk-thread, crotch and vine . . .
The sound of the belch'd words of my voice loos'd to the eddies of the wind.

This is self-delighting speech, a stroking of the voice's buzzy plosive vibrations. And Whitman offers his definition of this vocal aesthetic when he praises the 'full abandon and veracity of the farm-fields' in Burns's Scots vernacular and asks:

Is there not often something in the very neglect, unfinish, careless nudity, slovenly hiatus, coming from intrinsic genius and not 'put on', that secretly pleases the soul more than the wrought and re-wrought polish of the most perfect verse?

With some reservations Whitman is here recognizing the gnarled, spiky qualities of verse formed by writers nurtured in an oral community.

Until recently, many of the poets I have included in this anthology would have been termed 'dialect' poets – a term which works to marginalize regional speech and privilege Standard English. *Vernacular* is a term used in sociolinguistics to refer to 'the indigenous language or dialect of a speech community, e.g. the vernacular of Liverpool, Berkshire, Jamaica etc.'. The problem with the term *dialect* is that it has a certain archaic, quaint, over-baked remoteness that really belongs in the dead fragrance of a folk-museum. Yet those readers who dislike, say, Barnes's poetry might argue that his poems are merely the expression of a self-conscious and parochial antiquarianism. However, both Hopkins and Hardy admired and learnt from Barnes, and those three poets are kin with Whitman and Burns in a common family of vernacular writers. Such writers are linked by the way in which they employ language as speech process in their poems, not necessarily by their use of dialect words or regional accents – Christina Rossetti, for example, is one of the most significant members of this group of writers, yet she uses neither local accent nor *lexis* in her poems.

Hopkins admired Whitman's style for what he termed its 'savage' qualities, and in 'Inversnaid' he links this primitivist aesthetic to Scots:

> Degged with dew, dappled with dew
> Are the groins of the braes that the brook treads through,
> Wiry heathpacks, flitches of fern,
> And the beadbonny ash that sits over the burn.

The imagery of pubic hair echoes Whitman's 'silk-thread, crotch and vine', while the 'darksome burn' is a natural figure for Scottish speech, landscape, national poet. It's a wet wilderness which Hopkins imbues with mystery and violence – the liquid helter-skelter has a wild primitivist energy which 'treads' like a Highland clan loping down a brae into battle. Hopkins, like Whitman, aims to shock and he makes calculated use of what would elsewhere be termed 'bad taste'. This in some ways camp aesthetic joins tenderness with violence, as in Whitman's 'Wheeze, cluck, swash of falling blood, short wild scream, and long, dull, tapering groan'. Such fascination with violence is common to children's rhymes – Davy Crockett is admired because he polished off his mother when he was only three, then polished off his father with DDT.

For Burns and Whitman these savage vernacular energies are essentially democratic and Protestant. They can be imaged in the figure Browning terms 'grand rough old Martin Luther'. But for Hopkins Luther is the 'beast of the waste wood' and is associated with Protestant nationhood and an aggressive individualism. Hopkins is therefore torn between his dedication to popular speech and a knowledge that the native alliteration of his verse – its Germanic consonantal density – expresses a cultural atavism which he as a Catholic ought to reject.

The Nordic is central to the imagination of British Protestantism and it's celebrated in Hughes's 'Thistles' where the thistle-spikes thrust up like splintered weapons:

> From the underground stain of a decayed Viking.
> They are like pale hair and the gutturals of dialects.

The thistles are like 'Icelandic frost' and Hughes is here invoking ancestral energies similar to those Carlyle defines in *On Heroes, Hero-Worship and the Heroic in History*:

Frost the old Norse Seer discerns to be a monstrous hoary Jötum, the Giant *Thrym, Hrym*; or *Rime*, the old word now nearly obsolete here, but still used in Scotland to signify hoar-frost. *Rime* was not then as now a dead chemical thing, but a living Jötum or Devil . . .

Like John Thornton, the mill owner in Gaskell's *North and South* who asserts 'I belong to Teutonic blood', Hughes is firmly on the side of an energetic Protestant individualism. His reaction against the civil decencies of Movement verse and identification with what he elsewhere terms 'the iron blood of Calvin' make him a Thatcherite before Thatcher.

Hopkins observed the effects of the industrial revolution in northern England and was horrified by the poverty and suffering he saw, yet his poetic committed him to the Teutonic, the mill-building energies. He sought to subtilize the Anglo-Saxon inheritance through Celticism, Welsh vowel chimes, that Arthurian vision of Romano-Britain he invokes so desperately at the end of *The Wreck of the Deutschland*. He imagines a Celtic and Catholic, pre-imperial Britain, but he does so in a language still laced with a colonizing fire and stress.

Hopkins's term for the effect of spontaneous speech he seeks always in his verse was 'sprung rhythm'. He defined this rhythm as 'scanning by accents and syllables alone' – not counting up syllables – so that a foot could be 'one strong syllable' or 'many light and one strong'. He found hints of this rhythm in music, nursery rhymes, weather saws, popular jingles and in certain poets. Writing to R. W. Dixon, he said:

Here are instances – '*Díng, dóng, béll*; Pússy's ín the wéll; *Whó pút* her ín? Líttle Jóhnny Thín. *Whó púlled* her óut? Líttle Jóhnny Stóut.' For if each line has three stresses or three feet it follows that some of the feet are of one syllable only. So too '*Óne, twó*, Búckle my shóe' *passim*. In Campbell you have 'Ánd their fléet alóng the *déep próudly* shóne' – 'Ít was tén of Ápril *mórn bý* the chíme' etc; in Shakspere 'Whý shd. *thís* désert bé?' corrected wrongly by the editors . . .

For Hopkins, sprung rhythm is a bridge between common speech and the verse of certain poets who employ what Hardy termed the 'Gothic' architectural principle of 'spontaneity' and 'cunning irregularity'. Such poets aim to give their verse a stressed texture rather than a regular syllabic veneer, for they associate a polished rhythm with betrayal and insincerity. These poets ride the currents of exclamatory demotic speech – like Peter in Hardy's 'In the Servants' Quarters' they voice syllables as if they are 'talking unawares'.

These natural cadences can also be found in ballad rhythm, a rhythm which belongs to oral culture and is enlisted by Coleridge when he argues that the metre of 'Christabel' is not properly 'irregular'. His metre may seem so, he suggests, because it is founded on a new principle of counting the accents, not the syllables, in each line. The syllables may vary line by line from seven to twelve, yet each line will be found to contain only four accents. Reminding Hopkins of this principle, Dixon notes that Coleridge read some of Tennyson's early volumes and remarked that Tennyson did not understand versification:

The meaning of that utterance must have been that Tennyson's verse is (very often at least) strictly quantitative, each verse having the same number & disposition of syllables as its fellow in the staff. The most remarkable example of this is Locksley

Hall, which is without a flaw in this respect. I was reading it over the other day, & while it seemed a wonderfully ingenious piece of versification, wonderfully faithful to the rule which the writer had evidently put before him, yet I grew utterly satiate & weary with it, on this very account. It had the effect of being artificial & *light*: most unfit for intense passion, of which indeed there is nothing in it, but only a man making an unpleasant and rather ungentlemanly row. Tennyson is a great outsider.

Dixon did not realize that Hopkins admired the ungentlemanly or 'tykish', but his perception of the terrible hollow flaw in Tennyson's metric is exact and arresting, and it was shared by Hopkins. For most readers, though, Tennyson is the great insider, Hopkins the Victorian underdog who became a posthumous Modernist. But if Hopkins appears to exist underground in terms of nineteenth-century literary history, we should note that he belonged to that family of vernacular poets which includes Browning and Christina Rossetti – a poet badly neglected this century – as well as Burns, Whitman, Hardy.

Hopkins had a deep admiration for Rossetti, though he found Browning exasperating. And if Browning's vocal impersonations can often sound forced and ersatz, like hammy voices out of a costume drama, Rossetti's poems are always exactly keyed to the registers of the natural speaking voice:

> Her gleáming lócks shòwed nót òne thréad of gréy,
> Her bréath was swéet as Máy
> And líght dánced in her éyes.
>
> Dáys, wéeks, mónths, yéars
> Áfterwárds, when bóth were wíves . . .

Throughout *Goblin Market*, Rossetti varies stress and syllable count so that her lines correspond to Hopkins's definition of verse as 'figure of spoken sound'. Where Hopkins looked to existing nursery rhymes and weather saws, Rossetti both drew on that traditional oral culture and composed her own nursery rhymes. Some celebrate pure sound and rhythm – 'Kookoorookoo! kookoorookoo!' – while others show that animism and identification with living creatures and plants which is such a feature of the vernacular imagination – 'Brown and furry / caterpillar in a hurry'. Others react characteristically against the respectable and the official – 'I caught a little lady wife / That is both staid and gay.'

Rossetti's critique of Victorian patriarchy is evident in *Goblin Market* and in the much less well-known 'The Iniquity of the Fathers upon the Children', where the alienated female voice wants to reject her conventional social destiny:

> Perhaps the rising grazier,
> Or temperance publican,
> May claim my wifely duties.
> Meanwhile I wait their leisure
> And grace-bestowing pleasure,
> I wait the happy man;
> But if I hold my head
> And pitch my expectations
> Just higher than their level,
> They must fall back on patience:
> I may not mean to wed,
> Yet I'll be civil.

Margaret doesn't want to surrender her autonomy and she is able to stand outside her society with an almost clinical radicalism:

> Our one-street village stood
> A long mile from the town,
> A mile of windy down
> And bleak one-sided wood,
> With not a single house.
> Our town itself was small,
> With just the common shops,
> And throve in its small way.
> Our neighbouring gentry reared
> The good old-fashioned crops,
> And made old-fashioned boasts
> Of what John Bull would do
> If Frenchman Frog appeared,
> And drank old-fashioned toasts,
> And made old-fashioned bows
> To my Lady at the Hall.

The shifting accents play against the observed cultural clichés so that we perceive the enormous gulf between the intimate speaking voice and the threatening masculine cheeriness of village society. Rossetti's criticism of patriarchal values is expressed as much by her deployment of this subtle voice and metric as by what the voice states.

Although Rossetti, like Clough, writes in Standard English, both poets share that rejection of an imposed, normative official voice which is such a common feature of vernacular poetry. They refuse to recognize the division between 'serious' and 'light' verse which the vogue for dialect verse in the Victorian period helped to enforce. Yet if Tennyson kept Lincolnshire speech and the vowelly language of his other poems strictly separate, 'The Spinster's Sweet-Arts' is more than a comic exercise. Like Margaret in 'The Iniquity of the Fathers', the female speaker refuses to succumb to male domination, while her reference to babies' 'bottles o' pap, an' their mucky bibs, an' the clats an' the clouts' allows Tennyson to write more frankly than he could in the standard language. And that full veracious abandon can be found in the anonymous 'A Pitman's Love-song':

> Aw wish my lover was a ripe turd
> smoking doon in yon dyke seid
> an aw mysel was a shitten flee
> aw'd sook her allup before she was dreid

It's difficult to see how these lines could escape the often censoring effect of standard diction and accent.

Often regional English is charged with an erotic current – 'hold my bonnet hold my shawl / pray don't touch my waterfall', has to be voiced in black American English, while Whitman, like Dickinson, delights in the sensual nature of certain voices and sounds. Both poets, like Christopher Smart, like the anonymous voice of 'Oh trial!' or the equally anonymous Caribbean and communal 'Freedom A Come Oh!', witness to their experiences and beliefs in a distinctively Protestant, libertarian manner. Praising 'Nations, and languages, and every Creature, in which is the breath of Life', Smart aspires to a pure vernacular afflatus:

Let Anaiah bless with the Dragon-fly, who sails over the pond by the wood-side and feedeth on the cressies.

Like Burns's wee sleekit beastie or the animals and birds in Clare's poems, the dragon-fly and the cressies are not objects of empirical observation, but living, breathing parts of a more than personal vision. Lawrence draws marvellously on that close, sensitive, popular and native imagination in his depiction of Walter Morel in *Sons and Lovers* and in poems like 'Tortoise Shell' or 'Bare Almond-Trees'.

Sometimes the vernacular imagination confronts an aristocratic or public school voice directly:

> What I hated in those high soprano ranges
> was uplift beyond all reason and control

The particular voice Harrison hated was Hugh Gaitskell's, and the full patrician vowel can be irksome to those who prefer what Dryden termed 'our old Teuton monosyllables'. Yet in Clough's hexameters the range and limitations of that voice are beautifully dramatized when Claude says that Mrs Trevellyn

> Is – shall I call it fine? – herself she would tell you refined, and
> Greatly, I fear me, looks down on my bookish and maladroit manners;
> Somewhat affecteth the blue; would talk to me often of poets;
> Quotes, which I hate, Childe Harold; but also appreciates Wordsworth;
> Sometimes adventures on Schiller; and then to religion diverges;
> Questions me much about Oxford; and yet, in her loftiest flights, still
> Grates the fastidious ear with the slightly mercantile accent.

Claude is precise, refined, a snobbish aesthete irked by Mrs Trevellyn's still slightly middle-class accent. His hexameters have a Hellenic spontaneity of consciousness which is challenged by the Trevellyns' bourgeois Protestantism, their embodiment of what Clough's friend, Arnold, termed the 'Hebraic'. Claude's voice is exquisitely modulated, it ripples and hesitates, preens and soars with an apparently perfect confidence. But it's also the accent of a frightened phoney, a highly cultivated young man who is unable to feel or to telegram real love and anger.

Clough is fascinated by the speaking voice's deft stops and starts:

> Is it contemptible, Eustace, – I'm perfectly ready to think so, –
> Is it, – the horrible pleasure of pleasing inferior people?

This is the grammar of speech, and its baroque suddenness erupts in *The Wreck of the Deutschland* where Hopkins asks and exclaims

> But how shall I . . . make me room there:
> Reach me a . . . Fancy, come faster –
> Strike you the sight of it? look at it loom there,
> Thing that she . . . There then! the Master

These lines develop a technique initiated by Marlowe in Faustus's final soliloquy: 'See see where Christs blood streames in the firmament'. Faustus's speech resonates in Donne's religious verse and is echoed clumsily in Richard III's soliloquy before Bosworth. Marlowe's intense Protestant egotism enables a new poetry of consciousness, whose endlessly taut, swathing processes can be heard in the naked thinking voice of Lawrence's free verse: 'I say untarnished, but I mean opaque – '. Like Dickinson, Lawrence uses dashes to denote the postures of the speaking voice, and though he didn't share her puritan detestation of the codified formality of print, both poets are joined by a common cultural root – dissenting Protestantism. They aim to communicate an overwhelming sense of the present moment, the now of utterance:

> It's like the Light –
> A fashionless Delight –
> It's like the Bee –
> A dateless – Melody –

This is a language impatient of print, an orality that seeks to fly through its authoritarian nets.

Similarly the Baptist witness of 'Oh trial!' breaks with Anglican decorum to express a driven sense of mission and conviction:

> church light   church light
> church light till I die
> I been grown up in the church light side
> an die under church light rule
> oh trial!
> great trevelation children ho!
> trial!
> we bound t'leave dis world

This voice, like the Rastafarian voice in 'Africa me wan fe go / Africa me wan fe go', rejects the official order and seeks an alternative and juster society. It's a communal speech which articulates the violent displacement of slavery and colonialism, the experience of losing language and homeland and having another language – or bits of other languages – imposed on you:

> Come back to me
> my language.
> Come back,
> cacao,
> grigri,

> solitaire,
> ciseau
> the scissor-bird

Implicitly, Derek Walcott rejects the idea of linguistic purity – a racist idea expressed in Spenser's praise of Chaucer as the 'well of English undefiled' – and imagines a language which carries and breaks free from history, a language which exults in its mixing of different races and cultures.

John Clare's oral writings issue from the experience of a kind of internal colonialism – Enclosure – which traumatized him and led him to reject Anglicanism and become a Ranter. Clare felt robbed of his language and complained that 'grammer in learning is like Tyranny in government'. His publisher, John Taylor, urged him to get rid of oral 'provincialisms' in his poetry – for example, to substitute 'gush'd' for 'gulsh'd' or drop 'himsen'. Taylor edited, reshaped and sometimes rewrote Clare's unpunctuated poems so that Clare felt robbed of his ties to the land and to his native speech-community. The restored texts of the poems embody an alternative social idea. With their lack of punctuation, freedom from standard spelling and charged demotic ripples, they become a form of Nation Language that rejects the polished urbanity of Official Standard. They are communal speech – the speech of the Northamptonshire peasantry – vulnerable before the all-powerful language of aristocratic politicians and the printed language of parliamentary statutes.

Clare's biblical Protestantism, his Ranter's sense of being trapped within an unjust society and an authoritarian language, show in this letter he wrote from Northampton General Lunatic Asylum:

this is the English Bastile a government Prison where harmless people are trapped & tortured till they die – English priestcraft & english bondage more severe then the slavery of Egypt & Affrica

In his anguished madness, Clare dramatizes his experience of the class system and its codified language as exile and imprisonment in Babylon. He, too, is crying out 'Zion me wan go home'.

The voice of Babylon speaks in this contemporary review of Clare's *The Shepherd's Calendar*:

We had not, however, perused many pages before we discovered that our self-suspicions were wholly groundless. Wretched taste, poverty of thought, and unintelligible phraseology, for some time appeared its only characteristics. There was nothing, perhaps, which more provoked our spleen than the want of a glossary; for, without such assistance, how could we perceive the fitness and beauty of such words as – *crizzling* – *sliveth* – *whinneys* – *greening* – *tootles* – *croodling* – *hings* – *progged* – *spindling* – *siling* – *struttles* – &c. &c.

The italicized words each have that unique, one-off, familial rareness Muldoon celebrates in 'Quoof', but here they enter the language only to be expelled by the uptight efficient voice of Official Standard. These are homeless, evicted words powerlessly falling through a social void. And in 'The Lament of Swordy Well' the common land protests against this type of violent social and linguistic engineering. Many of Clare's poems are pitched against the Lockean idea of individualism, personal property, the view that words are merely flat functional signs. It's as if Clare, like a North American Indian, believes the land owns the people, instead of being owned by certain individuals.

From this point of view, printed language is alien, inauthentic and cruelly powerful. Print is a form of violence, its signs are like that 'curious T' which Pip's brain-damaged sister chalks on her slate in *Great Expectations*. In Dickens's novel, the letter *T*, a leg-iron and a hammer are identified – the *T* signifies Orlick who has felled Mrs Gargery with the leg-iron that clamped Magwitch's ankle. Dickens shows how the oral community which Mrs Gargery, Joe, Magwitch and initially Pip belong to is powerless before the force of print, the legal system, male violence and gentility.

Pip, like Clare, moves out of the oral community into the literate and hostile public world:

'mI deEr JO i opE U r krWitE wEll i opE i shAl soN B haBelL 4 2 teeDge U JO aN theN wE shOrl b sO glOdd aN wEn i M preNgtD 2 u JO woT larX an blEvE ME inF xn PiP.'

Pip's inscribed speech is poignant because it contains the threat of future alienation – Pip will one day become a chill and educated gentleman who snobbishly looks down on the illiterate Joe. Now, in the moment of the hearth's warmth, Joe doesn't understand that Pip will write himself out of their Edenic oral world. The hearth is covered with all the letters of the alphabet – death's signs have infiltrated the house. And even though it's a statement of his bond of love with Joe, Pip's slate symbolizes the decomposition of paradisal speech, the beginning of the Fall.

I have no wish to sentimentalize orality, only to notice that the vernacular imagination distrusts print in the way that most of us dislike legal documents. That imagination expresses itself in speech and feels trammelled by the monolithic simplicities of print, by those formulaic monotonies which distort the spirit of the living language. When I consider this – consider the way in which print-culture overrides local differences of speech and vocabulary – I recall a moment when that imagination spoke directly to me. I was out in a boat, lazily fishing for mackerel with a man I was fond of, an old merchant seaman from Islandmagee in Co. Antrim. He nodded up at the rainwashed, blue sky and said, 'D'you see thon wind-dog?' I looked up and saw a broken bit of rainbow and thought how rare and new 'wind-dog' seemed, how dull and beaten thin 'rainbow' was. It was MacDiarmid's 'chitterin' licht' of the watergaw just happening as he spoke.

It's from such moments that the inspiration for this anthology came. From an early age I became immersed in the wild dash and wit and loving playfulness of Northern Irish speech, a speech that is celebrated in Sally Belfrage's *The Crack*:

He hopped himself well up (dressed warmly) to go out for the messages (shopping). Then one thing led to another and all this caper and carry-on and whenever he stopped at the pub, he hoovered up five pints and got poleaxed (jarred, puddled, punctured, paladic, plucked, blocked, blitzed, snattered, stocious, steamboats, elephantsed, arsified, blootered, lockjawed, or merely full). 'You know what yer mon's like, like.' – 'Och aye. Not a titter of wit.' 'Did you get the sausingers but?' – 'I'm only after goin' til the shop so.'

In Robert Frost's terms, this is a speech packed with 'sentence sounds', sounds which writers gather 'by the ear from the vernacular'. Listening to a vocal phrase like 'Go you on back now' or 'I'll be with you in a minute but' or 'D'you see thon wind-dog?' I'm returned to Frost's aesthetic of the spoken word, to Huck's listening to those voices on the ferry landing, to these lines from a favourite Belfast street-song:

> my Aunt Jane has a bell on the door
> a white stone step and a clean swept floor
> candy apples   hard green pears
> conversation lozengers
> candy apples   hard green pears
> conversation lozengers

The lovely packed stresses – a whíte stóne stép and a cléan swépt flóor –

have an ecstatic tribal innocence that suddenly breaks the surface-rhythm like a shoal of fry. And deep down I hear a phrase in another stanza – 'three black lumps' – as '*th-ee* black lumps'. For a moment, Belfast's Ormeau Road is the omphalos of the universe, then those doubts some navel-gazers are prone to intervene . . . might a poem by Betjeman not be having the same effect elsewhere?

But in that moment what I discover is an entrance to that wild and perfect garden which is celebrated in naïf or primitive art. That art was a powerful influence on Elizabeth Bishop's writing, and her cherishing vernacular affirms its value in 'Crusoe in England' when Crusoe exclaims, 'Home-made, home-made!', and then adds, 'But aren't we all?'

It hasn't been my intention to gather a series of homey, self-conscious accents, but to show something of the intoxication of speech, its variety and crack and hilarity. Many of the voices that speak here are disaffected and powerless. They know that out in the public world a polished speech issues orders and receives deference. It seeks to flatten out and obliterate all the varieties of spoken English and to substitute one accent for all the others. It may be the ruin of us yet.

TOM PAULIN

Bairns and Wains

Tickle Talk

Tae titly
little fitty
shin sharpy
knee knapy
hinchie pinchy
wymie bulgy
breast berry
chin cherry
moo merry
nose nappy
ee winky
broo brinky
ower the croon
and awa wi it

Brow bender
eye peeper
nose deeper
mouth eater
chin chopper
knock at the door
ring the bell
lift up the latch
walk in
take a chair
sit by there
how dyou do this morning?

ANON

A Dandling Song

Dance to your daddy
my little babby
dance to your daddy
my little lamb
you shall have a fishy
in a little dishy
you shall have a fishy
when the boät comes in

ANON

Face Tapping

Here sits the lord mayor
here sit his men
here sits the cockadoodle
here sits the hen
here sit the little chickens
here they run in
chin chopper chin chopper chin chopper CHIN!

ANON

Ladybird 1

Ladybird ladybird
fly away home
your house is on fire
and your children all gone
all except one
and that's little Ann
and she has crept under
the warming pan

ANON

Ladybird 2

Cowlady cowlady
hie thy way wum
thy haase is afire
thy childer all gone
all but poor Nanny
set under a pan
weyvin gold lace
as fast as she can

ANON

'Dingty diddlety'

Dingty diddlety
my mammy's maid
she stole oranges
I am afraid
some in her pocket
and some in her sleeve
she stole oranges
I do believe

ANON

The Moon

Moon penny bright as silver
come and play with little childer

ANON

Tig

eeny meeny   figgety fig
ill doll   allymalig
blockety block   stony rock
hum bum thrush

ANON

Counting Out

1.
Inter mitzy titzy tool
ira dira dominu
oker poker dominoker
out goes you

2.
Intery mintery cutery corn
apple seed and briar thorn
wire briar limber lock
five geese in a flock
sit and sing by a spring
O U T and in again

ANON

Thread the Needle

Thread the needle   thread the needle
eye eye eye
thread the needle   thread the needle
eye eye eye

ANON

A Clapping Chant

Em pom pee para me
para moscas
em pom pee para me
acca dairy so fairy
acca dairy
poof poof!

ANON

Colon Bay

Me lover gone a Colon Bay
Colon Bay   Colon Bay
me lover gone a Colon Bay
with a handsome concentina
oh what is your intention
intention intention
oh what is your intention
my intention is to marry you
I will married to you I will married to you
I will married to you I will married to you
I will married to you I will married to you
with a handsome concentina
with a handsome concentina
IwillmarriedtoyouIwillmarriedtoyou
IwillmarriedtoyouIwillmarriedtoyou
withahandsomeconcentinawithahandsomecon-
  centina

ANON

Davy Crockett

Born on a tabletop in Joe's café
dirtiest place in the USA
polished off his father when he was only three
polished off his mother with DDT
Davy Davy Crockett
king of the wild frontier

ANON

'Draw a bucket of water'

Draw a bucket of water
for my lady's daughter
one in the tub   two in the tub
three in the tub   four in the tub
four little dollies in a rub a dub dub
four little dollies in a rub dub dub

ANON

Dry River

guava

You no give me one wacky you can't pass
you no give me one wacky you can't pass
you no give me one wacky you can't pass
Dry River will come an take you way
draw me nearer
draw me near
Dry River will come an take you way

ANON

The Candy Man

The candy man was guid tae me
he took me up and gied me tea —
tea and toast an a wee bit ham
twas afa guid o'the candy man

ANON

Lubin

Here we come looby loo
here we come looby light
here we come looby loo
all on a Saturday night

Put your right hand in
put your right hand out
shake it little by little
and turn yourself about

ANON

The Wind Blows High

The wind the wind the wind blows high
the rain comes scattering down the sky
she is handsome she is pretty
she is the girl of the golden city
she goes acourting one two three
please and tell me who is she

Gerry Johnson says he loves her
all the boys are fighting for her
let the boys say what they will
Gerry Johnson loves her still

he loves her he kisses her he sets her on his knee
he says dear darling won't you marry me?
he says tomorrow and she says today
so let's get a taxi and drive them away

ANON

My Aunt Jane

My Aunt Jane she took me in
she give me sweets outa her wee tin
half a bap   sugar on the top
three black lumps outa her wee shop
half a bap   sugar on the top
three black lumps outa her wee shop

my Aunt Jane she's awful smart
she bakes wee rings in an apple tart
and when Halloween comes round
next to fornenst that tart I'm always found
and when Halloween comes round
fornenst that tart I'm always found

my Aunt Jane has a bell on the door
a white stone step and a clean swept floor
candy apples   hard green pears
conversation lozengers
candy apples   hard green pears
conversation lozengers

ANON

London Bridge

London Bridge is broken down
grand says the little bee
London Bridge is broken down
where I'd be

Stones and lime will build it up
grand says the little bee
stones and lime will build it up
where I'd be

Get a man to watch all night
grand says the little bee
get a man to watch all night
where I'd be

Perhaps that man might fall asleep
grand says the little bee
perhaps that man might fall asleep
where I'd be

Get a dog to watch all night
grand said the little bee
get a dog to watch all night
where I'd be

If that dog should run away
grand said the little bee
if that dog should run away
where I'd be

Give that dog a bone to pick
grand said the little bee
give that dog a bone to pick
where I'd be

ANON

The Big Ship Sails

The big ship sails on the alley alley oh
the alley alley oh   the alley alley oh
the big ship sails on the alley alley oh
on the last day of September

we all dip our hands in the deep blue sea
the deep blue sea   the deep blue sea
we all dip our hands in the deep blue sea
on the last day of September

The captain said this will never never do
never never do   never never do
the captain said this will never never do
on the last day of September

ANON

'Draw a pail of water'

Draw a pail of water
for my ladys daughter
my fathers a king and my mothers a queen
my two little sisters are dressed in green
stamping grass and parsley
marigold leaves and daisies
one rush two rush
pray thee fine lady come under my bush

ANON

'Cuckoo cherry tree'

Cuckoo cherry tree
lay an egg give it me
lay another
give it my brother!

ANON

We Three Kings

We three kings all orient are
one in a taxi one in a car
one on a scooter blowing his hooter
smoking a big cigar

oh star of wonder star of bright
sit on a box of dynamite
light the fuse and off we go
all the way to Mexico

ANON

Under the Bram Bush

Under the bram bush
under the sea   boom boom boom
true love for you my darling
true love for me
when we get married
we'll have a family
a boy for you   a girl for me
um tiddley um dum   SEXY!

ANON

Latin

Latin is a dead tongue
dead as dead can be
first it killed the Romans
now it's killing me
all are dead who wrote it
all are dead who spoke it
all are dead who learnt it
lucky dead they've earnt it

ANON

Birds, Beasties, Bugs

The Cuckoo

In the month of Averil
the gowk comes over the hill
in a shower of rain

ANON

Pewits Nest

Accross the fallow clods at early morn
I took a random track where scant and spare
The grass and nibbled leaves all closely shorn
Leaves a burnt flat all bleaching brown and bare
Where hungry sheep in freedom range forlorn
And neath the leaning willow and odd thorn
And molehill large that vagrant shade supplies
They batter round to shun the teazing flies
Trampling smooth places hard as cottage floors
Where the time killing lonely shepherd boys
Whose summer homes are ever out of doors
Their chock holes form and chalk their marble
    ring
marbles   And make their clay taws at the bubbling spring
And in their wrangling sport and gambling joys
stride   They strime their clock like shadows – when it
    cloys
To guess the hour that slowly runs away
And shorten sultry turmoil with their play

Here did I roam while veering over head
The pewet whirred in many whewing rings
And 'chewsit' screamed and clapped her flopping
    wings
To hunt her nest my rambling steps was led
Oer the broad baulk beset with little hills
By moles long formed and pismires tennanted

As likely spots but still I searched in vain
When all at once the noisey birds were still
And on the lands a furrowed ridge between
Chance found four eggs of dingy olive green
Deep blotched with plashy spots of jockolate stain
Their small ends inward turned as ever found
As though some curious hand had laid them round
Yet lying on the ground with nought at all
Of soft grass withered twitch and bleached weed
To keep them from the rain storms frequent fall
And here she broods on her unsavoury bed
When bye and bye with little care and heed
Her young with each a shell upon its head
Run after their wild parents restless cry
And from their own fears tiney shadows run
Neath clods and stones to cringe and snugly lie
Hid from all sight but the allseeing sun
Till never ceasing danger seemeth bye

JOHN CLARE

The Three Puddocks

Three wee bit puddocks
Sat upon a stane:
Tick-a-tack, nick-a-nack,
collar-bone   Brek your hawse-bane.
muddy pond   They lookit in a dub
And made nae sound
stars   For they saw a' the sterns
whirling   Gang whummlin round.

Then ane lauch't a lauch
Gowpin wide his gab,
And plunkit doun into the dub
But naething cud he nab:
mouthful of mud   And wi' a mou o' mools
drenched   He cam droukit out again:
Tick-a-tack, nick-a-nack,
Brek your hawse-bane.

Anither lauch't a lauch
fools / swim   (Wha but gowks wud soom)
perched / knoll   And cockit on his stany knowe
Afore the dub wud toom;
slime   Then he growpit in the glaur
Whaur he thocht the sterns had gaen:
Tick-a-tack, nick-a-nack,
Brek your hawse-bane.

The hinmaist lauch't a lauch,
throwing / head   Coostin up his croun;
And richt into his liftit e'en
The sterns were lauchin doun.
whistling   Cauld, cauld, the wheeplin wind;
big   Cauld the muckle stane:
Tick-a-tack, nick-a-nack,
Brek your hawse-bane.

WILLIAM SOUTAR

To a Mouse

On Turning Her Up in Her Nest,
with the Plough, November 1785

Wee, sleekit, cowrin, tim'rous beastie,
O, what a panic's in thy breastie!
Thou need na start awa sae hasty,
scamper   Wi' bickering brattle!
I wad be laith to rin an' chase thee,
plough-staff   Wi' murd'ring pattle!

I'm truly sorry Man's dominion
Has broken Nature's social union,
An' justifies that ill opinion,
                    Which makes thee startle,
At me, thy poor, earth-born companion,
                    An' fellow-mortal!

sometimes   I doubt na, whyles, but thou may thieve;
What then? poor beastie, thou maun live!
odd ear in a couple of stooks A daimen icker in a thrave
                    'S a sma' request.
what's left   I'll get a blessin wi' the lave,
                    An' never miss't!

Thy wee-bit housie, too, in ruin!
feeble   Its silly wa's the win's are strewin!
build   An' naething, now, to big a new ane,
moss   O' foggage green!
An' bleak December's winds ensuin,
biting   Baith snell an' keen!

Thou saw the fields laid bare an' waste,
An' weary Winter comin fast,
An' cozie here, beneath the blast,
   Thou thought to dwell,

iron cutter on plough Till crash! the cruel coulter past
     Out thro' thy cell.

That wee-bit heap o' leave an' stibble
Has cost thee monie a weary nibble!
Now thou's turn'd out, for a' thy trouble,
    But house or hald,

without house or holding

endure To thole the Winter's sleety dribble,

hoar-frost   An' cranreuch cauld!

alone But, Mousie, thou art no thy lane,
In proving foresight may be vain:
The best-laid schemes o' Mice an' Men
    Gang aft a-gley,

awry An' lea'e us nought but grief an' pain,
    For promis'd joy!

Still thou art blest, compar'd wi' me!
The present only toucheth thee:
But, Och! I backward cast my e'e
    On prospects drear!
An' forward, tho' I canna see,
    I guess an' fear!

ROBERT BURNS

The Badger

The badger grunting on his woodland track
marked in lines
With shaggy hide and sharp nose scrowed with
  black
Roots in the bushes and the woods and makes
A great hugh burrow in the ferns and brakes
With nose on ground he runs a awkard pace
And anything will beat him in the race
The shepherds dog will run him to his den
Followed and hooted by the dogs and men
The woodman when the hunting comes about
Go round at night to stop the foxes out
And hurrying through the bushes ferns and
  brakes
Nor sees the many holes the badger makes
And often through the bushes to the chin
Breaks the old holes and tumbles headlong in

When midnight comes a host of dogs and men
Go out and track the badger to his den
And put a sack within the hole and lye
Till the old grunting badger passes bye
He comes and hears they let the strongest loose
The old fox hears the noise and drops the goose
The poacher shoots and hurrys from the cry
And the old hare half wounded buzzes bye
They get a forked stick to bear him down
And clapt the dogs and bore him to the town
And bait him all the day with many dogs
And laugh and shout and fright the scampering
  hogs
He runs along and bites at all he meets
They shout and hollo down the noisey streets

He turns about to face the loud uproar
And drives the rebels to their very doors
The frequent stone is hurled where ere they go
When badgers fight and every ones a foe
The dogs are clapt and urged to join the fray
The badger turns and drives them all away
Though scarcely half as big dimute and small
He fights with dogs for hours and beats them all
The heavy mastiff savage in the fray
Lies down and licks his feet and turns away
The bull dog knows his match and waxes cold
The badger grins and never leaves his hold
He drives the crowd and follows at their heels
And bites them through the drunkard swears and
   reels

The frighted women takes the boys away
The blackguard laughs and hurrys on the fray
He trys to reach the woods a awkard race
But sticks and cudgels quickly stop the chace
He turns agen and drives the noisey crowd
And beats the many dogs in noises loud
He drives away and beats them every one
And then they loose them all and set them on
He falls as dead and kicked by boys and men
Then starts and grins and drives the crowd agen
Till kicked and torn and beaten out he lies
And leaves his hold and cackles groans and dies

Some keep a baited badger tame as hog
And tame him till he follows like the dog
They urge him on like dogs and show fair play
He beats and scarcely wounded goes away
Lapt up as if asleep he scorns to fly
And siezes any dog that ventures nigh
Clapt like a dog he never bites the men
But worrys dogs and hurrys to his den
They let him out and turn a barrow down

And there he fights the pack of all the town
He licks the patting hand and trys to play
And never trys to bite or run away
And runs away from noise in hollow trees
Burnt by the boys to get a swarm of bees

JOHN CLARE

The Wee Jenny Wren

The wee jenny wren she lays sixteen
and brings them out both neat and clean
the scabby cuckoo she lays but two
and brings them out with enough to do

ANON

Mountain Lion

Climbing through the January snow, into the
    Lobo Canyon
Dark grow the spruce-trees, blue is the balsam,
    water sounds still unfrozen, and the trail is still
    evident.

Men!
Two men!
Men! The only animal in the world to fear!

They hesitate.
We hesitate.
They have a gun.
We have no gun.

Then we all advance, to meet.

Two Mexicans, strangers, emerging out of the
    dark and snow and inwardness of the Lobo
    valley.
    What are they doing here on this vanishing
    trail?

What is he carrying?
Something yellow.
A deer?

Qué tiene, amigo?
León –

He smiles, foolishly, as if he were caught doing
    wrong.
And we smile, foolishly, as if we didn't know.
He is quite gentle and dark-faced.

It is a mountain lion,
A long, long slim cat, yellow like a lioness.
Dead.

He trapped her this morning, he says, smiling
    foolishly.
Lift up her face,
Her round, bright face, bright as frost.
Her round, fine-fashioned head, with two dead
    ears;
And stripes in the brilliant frost of her face,
    sharp, fine dark rays,
Dark, keen, fine rays in the brilliant frost of her
    face.
Beautiful dead eyes.

Hermoso es!

They go out towards the open;
We go on into the gloom of Lobo.
And above the trees I found her lair,
A hole in the blood-orange brilliant rocks that
    stick up, a little cave.
And bones, and twigs, and a perilous ascent.

So, she will never leap up that way again, with
    the yellow flash of a mountain lion's long
    shoot!
And her bright striped frost-face will never watch
    any more, out of the shadow of the cave in the
    blood-orange rock,
Above the trees of the Lobo dark valley-mouth!

Instead, I look out.
And out to the dim of the desert, like a dream,
    never real;
To the snow of the Sangre de Cristo mountains,
    the ice of the mountains of Picoris,
And near across at the opposite steep of snow,
    green trees motionless standing in snow, like a
    Christmas toy.

And I think in this empty world there was room
    for me and a mountain lion.
And I think in the world beyond, how easily we
    might spare a million or two of humans
And never miss them.
Yet what a gap in the world, the missing white
    frost-face of that slim yellow mountain lion!
                                                            Lobo

D. H. LAWRENCE

The Hunting of the Hare

Betwixt two Ridges of Plowd-land, lay Wat,
Whose Body press'd to th'Earth lay close, and
   squat.
His Nose upon his two Fore-feet close lies,
Glaring obliquely with his great gray Eyes.
His Head he alwaies sets against the Wind;
If turne his Taile, his Haires blow up behind:
Which he too cold will grow, but he is wise,
And keeps his Coat still downe, so warm he lies.
Thus rests he all the day, still th'Sun doth set,
Then up he riseth his Reliefe to get,
And walks about untill the Sun doth rise,
Then back returnes, downe in his Forme he lyes.
At last, Poore Wat was found, as he there lay,
By Hunts-men, with their Dogs which came that
   way
Whom seeing, he got up, and fast did run,
Hoping some waies the Cruell Dogs to shun.
But they by Nature have so quick a Sent,
That by their Nose they trace what way he went.
And with their deep, wide Mouths set forth a
   Cry,
Which answer'd was by Ecchoes in the Skie.
Then Wat was struck with Terrour, and with
   Feare,
Thinkes every Shadow still the Dogs they were.
And running out some distance from the noise,
To hide himselfe, his Thoughts he new imploies.
Under a Clod of Earth in Sand-pit wide,
Poore Wat sat close, hoping himselfe to hide.
There long he had not been, but strait his Eares
The Winding Hornes, and crying Dogs he heares:
Then starting up with Feare, he leap'd, and such
   Swift speed he made, the Ground he scarce did
   touch;

UXBRIDGE COLLEGE LIBRARY

Into a great thick Wood he strait way gets,
Where underneath a broken Bough he sits.
At every Leafe that with the wind did shake,
Did bring such Terrour, made his Heart to ake.
That Place he left, to Champian Plaines he went,
Winding about, for to deceive their Sent.
And while they snuffling were, to find his Track,
Poore Wat, being weary, his swift pace did slack.
On his two hinder legs for ease did sit,
His Fore-feet rub'd his Face from Dust, and
    Sweat.
Licking his Feet, he wip'd his Eares so cleane,
That none could tell that Wat had hunted been.
But casting round about his faire great Eyes,
The Hounds in full Careere he neere him 'spies:
To Wat it was so terrible a Sight,
Feare gave him Wings, and made his Body light.
Though weary was before, by running long,
Yet now his Breath he never felt more strong.
Like those that dying are, think Health returns,
When tis but a faint Blast, which Life out burnes.
For Spirits seek to guard the Heart about,
Striving with Death, but Death doth quench them
    out.
The Hounds so fast came on, and with such Cry,
That he no hopes hath left, nor help could 'spy.
With that the Winds did pity poore Wats case,
And with their Breath the Sent blew from the
    Place.
Then every Nose is busily imployed,
And every Nostrill is set open, wide:
And every Head doth seek a severall way,
To find the Grasse, or Track where the Sent lay.
For witty industry is never slack,
'Tis like to Witchery and brings lost things back.
For though the Wind had tied the Sent up close,
A Busie Dog thrust in his Snuffling Nose:
And drew that out, with it did foremost run,

Then Hornes blew loud, for th'rest to follow on.
The great slow-Hounds, their throats did set a
    Base,
The Fleet Swift Hounds, as Tenours next in
    place;
The little Beagles did a Trebble sing,
And through the Aire their Voices round did ring
Which made such Consort, as they ran along;
That, had they spoken Words, t'had been a Song,
The Hornes kept time, the Hunters shout for Joy,
And seem'd most Valiant, poor Wat to destroy:
Spurring their Horses to a full Careere,
Swim Rivers deep, leap Ditches without feare;
Indanger Life, and Limbes, so fast will ride,
Onely to see how patiently Wat died.
For why, the Dogs so neere his Heeles did get,
That their sharp Teeth they in his Breech did set.
Then tumbling downe, did fall with weeping
    Eyes,
Gives up his Ghost, and thus poore Wat he dies.
Men hooping loud, such Acclamations make,
As if the Devill they did Prisoner take.
When they do but a shiftlesse Creature kill;
To hunt, there needs no Valiant Souldiers skill.
But Man doth think that Exercise, and Toile,
To keep their Health, is best, which makes most
    spoile.
Thinking that Food, and Nourishment so good,
And Appetite, that feeds on Flesh, and Blood.
When they do Lions, Wolves, Beares, Tigers see,
To kill poore Sheep, strait say, they cruell be.
But for themselves all Creatures think too few,
For Luxury, wish God would make more new.
As if God did make Creatures for Mans meat,
To give them Life, and Sense, for Man to eat;
Or else for Sport, or Recreations sake,
Destroy those Lifes that God saw good to make:

Making their Stomacks, Graves, which full they
    fill
With Murther'd Bodies, that in sport they kill.
Yet Man doth think himselfe so gentle, mild,
When of all Creatures he's most cruell wild.
And is so Proud, thinks onely he shall live,
That God a God-like Nature him did give.
And that all Creatures for his sake alone,
Was made for him, to Tyrannize upon.

MARGARET CAVENDISH, DUCHESS OF NEWCASTLE

Three Nursery Rhymes

Dead in the cold, a song-singing thrush,
Dead at the foot of a snowberry bush, –
Weave him a coffin of rush,
Dig him a grave where the soft mosses grow,
Raise him a tombstone of snow.

*

Brown and furry
Caterpillar in a hurry,
Take your walk
To the shady leaf, or stalk,
Or what not,
Which may be the chosen spot.
No toad spy you,
Hovering bird of prey pass by you;
Spin and die,
To live again a butterfly.

*

'Kookoorookoo! kookoorookoo!'
    Crows the cock before the morn;
'Kikirikee! kikirikee!'
    Roses in the east are born.

'Kookoorookoo! kookoorookoo!'
    Early birds begin their singing;
'Kikirikee! kikirikee!'
    The day, the day, the day is springing.

CHRISTINA ROSSETTI

Turkeys

The turkeys wade the close to catch bees
In the old border full of maple trees
And often lay away and breed and come

chirping   And bring a brood of chelping chickens home
The turkey gobbles loud and drops his rag

spreads out suddenly   And struts and sprunts his tail and drags
His wing on ground and makes a huzzing noise

raises himself   Nauntles at passer bye and drives the boys
And bounces up and flyes at passer bye
The old dogs snaps and grins nor ventures nigh
He gobbles loud and drives the boys from play
They throw their sticks and kick away
And turn agen the stone comes huzzing bye
He drops his quiet tail and forced to flye

Draws up his scarlet snout and cools to grey
And drops his gobble noise and sneaks away
He drives the noisey ducks as soon as loose
And fights with awkard haste the hissing goose
And tramples round and fairly beats him down
And quarrels with the maidens sunday gown
He often gives the cock and hens the chase
And drives the stranger till he leaves the place
And runs and gobbles up and when he beats
They all come up and follow the retreat
And when a beggar comes he nauntling steals
And gobbles loud and pecks the strangers heels

He fights the dunghill cock that quarrels hard
And hobbles round the master of the yard

The idle turkey gobbling half the day
Goes hobbling through the grass and lays away
Five and red spotted eggs where many pass
But none ere think of turkeys in the grass
The old dogs sees her on and goes away
The old dame calls and wonders where they lay
Among the old and thickest grass they lie
The fox unnotices and passes bye
The blackbird breeds above a cunning guest
And hides the shells cause none should find the nest
The old crow crawks around them every day
And trys to steal the turkeys eggs away
The magpie cackles around for any prey
And finds the wounded snake and goes away

JOHN CLARE

To a Louse, On Seeing one on a Lady's Bonnet at Church

creeping/marvel

Ha! whare ye gaun, ye crowlin' ferlie!
Your impudence protects you sairly:

strut

I canna say but ye strunt rarely,
      Owre gawze and lace;
Though faith, I fear ye dine but sparely,
      On sic a place.

wonder

Ye ugly, creepin' blastet wonner,
Detested, shunned, by saunt an' sinner,

foot

How daur ye set your fit upon her,
      Sae fine a lady!
Gae somewhere else and seek your dinner
      On some poor body.

Quick / lock of hair   Swith, in some beggar's haffet squattle;

scramble   There ye may creep, and sprawl, and sprattle,

Wi' ither kindred, jumping cattle,
              In shoals and nations;
Whare horn nor bane ne'er daur unsettle
              Your thick plantations.

Now haud you there, ye're out o' sight,

ribbons   Below the fatt'rels, snug and tight,

Na faith ye yet! ye'll no be right,
              Till ye've got on it,
The vera tapmost, towrin height
              O' Miss's bonnet.

My sooth! right bauld ye set your nose out,

gooseberry   As plump an' gray as onie grozet:

resin   O for some rank, mercurial rozet,

powder   Or fell, red smeddum,

I'd gie you sic a hearty dose o't,

backside   Wad dress your droddum!

I wad na been surprized to spy

flannel cap   You on an auld wife's flainen toy;

possibly / ragged   Or aiblins some bit duddie boy,

vest   On 's wylecoat;

bonnet   But Miss's fine Lunardi, fie!
              How daur ye do 't?

O Jenny, dinna toss your head,
An' set your beauties a' abread!
Ye little ken what cursed speed

nasty creature   The blastie's makin!

Thae winks and finger-ends, I dread,
              Are notice takin!

O wad some pow'r the giftie gie us
To see oursels as others see us!
It wad frae monie a blunder free us
          An' foolish notion:
What airs in dress an' gait wad lea'e us,
          And ev'n devotion!

ROBERT BURNS

Tortoise Shell

The Cross, the Cross
Goes deeper in than we know,
Deeper into life;
Right into the marrow
And through the bone.

Along the back of the baby tortoise
The scales are locked in an arch like a bridge,
Scale-lapping, like a lobster's sections
Or a bee's.
Then crossways down his sides
Tiger-stripes and wasp-bands.

Five, and five again, and five again,
And round the edges twenty-five little ones,
The sections of the baby tortoise shell.

Four, and a keystone;
Four, and a keystone;
Four, and a keystone;
Then twenty-four, and a tiny little keystone.

It needed Pythagoras to see life playing with
    counters on the living back
Of the baby tortoise;
Life establishing the first eternal mathematical
    tablet
Not in stone, like the Judean Lord, or bronze,
    but in life-clouded, life-rosy tortoise shell.

The first little mathematical gentleman
Stepping, wee mite, in his loose trousers
Under all the eternal dome of mathematical law.

Fives, and tens,
Threes and fours and twelves,
All the *volte face* of decimals,
The whirligig of dozens and the pinnacle of
    seven.

Turn him on his back,
The kicking little beetle,
And there again, on his shell-tender, earth-
    touching belly,
The long cleavage of division, upright of the
    eternal cross
And on either side count five,
On each side, two above, on each side, two
    below
The dark bar horizontal.

The Cross!
struggling　　It goes right through him, the sprottling insect,
Through his cross-wise cloven psyche,
Through his five-fold complex-nature.

So turn him over on his toes again;
Four pin-point toes; and a problematical thumb-
    piece,
Four rowing limbs, and one wedge-balancing
    head,

Four and one makes five, which is the clue to all
   mathematics.

The Lord wrote it all down on the little slate
Of the baby tortoise.
Outward and visible indication of the plan
   within,
The complex, manifold involvedness of an
   individual creature
Plotted out
On this small bird, this rudiment,
This little dome, this pediment
Of all creation,
This slow one.

D. H. LAWRENCE

The Green Woodpecker's Nest

The green woodpecker flying up and down
With wings of mellow green and speckled crown
She bores a hole in trees with crawking noise
And pelted down and often catched by boys
She makes a lither nest of grass and whool
Men fright her oft that go the sticks to pull
Ive up and clumb the trees with hook and pole
And stood on rotten grains to reach the hole
And as I trembled upon fear and doubt
I found the eggs and scarce could get them out
I put them in my hat a tattered crown
And scarcely without breaking brought them
   down
The eggs are small for such a bird they lay
Five eggs and like the sparrows spotted grey

supple

JOHN CLARE

Celebrations

Quaco Sam

When the rain an the breeze an the storm an the
    sun
I never see a man like a Quaco Sam
he live in the sun as well as the rain
I never see a man like a Quaco Sam
Quaco Sam was a little bitta man
I never see a man like a Quaco Sam
for he never build a house but he live as any man
I never see a funny man as Quaco Sam

ANON

The Bonnie Broukit Bairn

neglected

For Peggy

handsome/crimson

Mars is braw in crammasy,
Venus in a green silk goun,
The auld mune shak's her gowden feathers,
pack of nonsense Their starry talk's a wheen o' blethers,
Nane for thee a thochtie sparin',
Earth, thou bonnie broukit bairn!
weep — *But greet, an' in your tears ye'll droun*
mob *The haill clanjamfrie!*

HUGH MACDIARMID

Indian Bagman's Toast

Shearer man like toast and butter
Wolseley comb and Lister cutter
handyman   rouseabout like plenty joke
plenty rain and engine broke

ANON

Storm in the Black Forest

Now it is almost night, from the bronzey soft sky
jugfull after jugfull of pure white liquid fire,
    bright white
tipples over and spills down,
and is gone
and gold-bronze flutters bent through the thick
    upper air.

And as the electric liquid pours out, sometimes
a still brighter white snake wriggles among it,
    spilled
and tumbling wriggling down the sky:
and then the heavens cackle with uncouth
    sounds.

And the rain won't come, the rain refuses to
    come!

This is the electricity that man is supposed to
    have mastered
chained, subjugated to his use!
supposed to!

D. H. LAWRENCE

Gud Ber

Her I was and her I drank
farwyll dam and mykyll thank
her I was and had gud cher
and her I drank wyll gud ber

ANON

To a Haggis

good-natured

Fair fa' your honest, sonsie face,
Great Chieftan o' the Puddin-race!
Aboon them a' ye tak your place,

inferior dishes

Painch, tripe, or thairm:
Weel are ye wordy of a *grace*
As lang's my arm.

buttocks

skewer

The groaning trencher there ye fill,
Your hurdies like a distant hill,
Your *pin* wad help to mend a mill
In time o' need,
While thro' your pores the dews distil
Like amber bead.

His knife see Rustic-labour dight,
An' cut you up wi' ready slight,
Trenching your gushing entrails bright
Like onie ditch;
And then, O what a glorious sight,
Warm-reekin, rich!

Then, horn for horn they stretch an' strive,
Deil tak the hindmost, on they drive,
bellies/soon Till a' their weel-swall'd kytes belyve
     Are bent like drums;
burst Then auld Guidman, maist like to rive,
     Bethankit hums.

Is there that owre his French *ragout*,
poison Or *olio* that wad staw a sow,
Or *fricassee* wad mak her spew
disgust   Wi' perfect sconner,
Looks down wi' sneering, scornfu' view
     On sic a dinner?

Poor devil! see him owre his trash,
rush As feckless as a wither'd rash,
His spindle shank a guid whip-lash,
fist/nut   His nieve a nit;
Thro' bluidy flood or field to dash,
     O how unfit!

But mark the Rustic, *haggis-fed*,
The trembling earth resounds his tread,
ample Clap in his walie nieve a blade,
     He'll mak it whissle;
lop An' legs, an' arms, an' heads will sned,
thistle   Like taps o' thrissle.

Ye Pow'rs wha mak mankind your care,
And dish them out their bill o' fare,
watery Auld Scotland wants nae skinking ware
splashes/wooden dish   That jaups in luggies;
But, if ye wish her gratefu' pray'r,
     Gie her a *Haggis*!

ROBERT BURNS

Medlars and Sorb-Apples

I love you, rotten,
Delicious rottenness.

I love to suck you out from your skins
So brown and soft and coming suave,
So morbid, as the Italians say.

What a rare, powerful, reminiscent flavour
Comes out of your falling through the stages of
    decay:
Stream within stream.

Something of the same flavour of Syracusan
    muscat wine
Or vulgar Marsala.
Though even the word Marsala will smack of
    preciosity
Soon in the pussyfoot West.

What is it?
What is it, in the grape turning raisin,
In the medlar, in the sorb-apple,
Wineskins of brown morbidity,
Autumnal excrementa;
What is that reminds us of white gods?

Gods nude as blanched nut-kernels,
Strangely, half-sinisterly flesh-fragrant
As if with sweat,
And drenched with mystery.

Sorb-apples, medlars with dead crowns.
I say, wonderful are the hellish experiences,
Orphic, delicate
Dionysos of the Underworld.

A kiss, and a spasm of farewell, a moment's
     orgasm of rupture,
Then along the damp road alone, till the next
     turning.
And there, a new partner, a new parting, a new
     unfusing into twain,
A new gasp of further isolation,
A new intoxication of loneliness, among
     decaying, frost-cold leaves.

Going down the strange lanes of hell, more and
     more intensely alone,
The fibres of the heart parting one after the other
And yet the soul continuing, naked-footed, ever
     more vividly embodied
Like a flame blown whiter and whiter
In a deeper and deeper darkness
Ever more exquisite, distilled in separation.

So, in the strange retorts of medlars and sorb-
     apples
The distilled essence of hell.
The exquisite odour of leave-taking.
          Jamque vale!
Orpheus, and the winding, leaf-clogged, silent
     lanes of hell.

Each soul departing with its own isolation,
Strangest of all strange companions,
And best.

Medlars, sorb-apples,
More than sweet
Flux of autumn
Sucked out of your empty bladders

And sipped down, perhaps, with a sip of Marsala
So that the rambling, sky-dropped grape can add
    its savour to yours,
Orphic farewell, and farewell, and farewell
And the *ego sum* of Dionysos
The *sono io* of perfect drunkenness
Intoxication of final loneliness.

                                        San Gervasio

D. H. LAWRENCE

On an Island

You've plucked a curlew, drawn a hen,
Washed the shirts of seven men,
You've stuffed my pillow, stretched the sheet,
And filled the pan to wash your feet,
You've cooped the pullets, wound the clock,
And rinsed the young men's drinking crock;
And now we'll dance to jigs and reels,
Nailed boots chasing girls' naked heels,
Until your father'll start to snore,
And Jude, now you're married, will stretch on
    the floor.

J. M. SYNGE

To my Booke

It will be look'd for, booke, when some but see
    Thy title, *Epigrammes*, and nam'd of mee,
Thou should'st be bold, licentious, full of gall,
    Wormewood, and sulphure, sharpe, and
                                tooth'd withall;
Become a petulant thing, hurle inke, and wit,
    As mad-men stones: not caring whom they hit.

Deceive their malice, who could wish it so.
   And by thy wiser temper, let men know
Thou are not covetous of least selfe-fame,
   Made from the hazard of anothers shame:
Much lesse with lewd, prophane, and beastly
                    phrase,
   To catch the worlds loose laughter, or vaine
                    gaze.
He that departs with his owne honesty
   For vulgar praise, doth it too dearely buy.

BEN JONSON

First Time In

After the dread tales and red yarns of the Line
Anything might have come to us; but the divine
Afterglow brought us up to a Welsh colony
Hiding in sandbag ditches, whispering
   consolatory
Soft foreign things. Then we were taken in
To low huts candle-lit, shaded close by slitten
Oilsheets, and there the boys gave us kind
   welcome,
So that we looked out as from the edge of home,
Sang us Welsh things, and changed all former
   notions
To human hopeful things. And the next day's
   guns
Nor any line-pangs ever quite could blot out
That strangely beautiful entry to war's rout;
Candles they gave us, precious and shared over-
   rations –
Ulysses found little more in his wanderings
   without doubt.
'David of the White Rock', the 'Slumber Song' so
   soft, and that

Beautiful tune to which roguish words by Welsh
   pit boys
Are sung – but never more beautiful than there
   under the guns' noise.

IVOR GURNEY

Owdham Footbo'

It's run an' jump an' hop an' skip,
An' sheawt hooray, an' hip, hip, hip,
It's singin' songs an' eytin tripe,
An' suppin' pints at single swipe,
An' brass for th' wife to buy a hat,
An' th' childer brass for this an' that,
An' beauncin' gaily up an' deawn,
Yo' connut find a merrier teawn,
When Owdham's won.

bad-tempered   Aw lost mi brass, awm crabbed an' croat,
Aw lifted th' cat eawt wi' mi boot,
Awr ne'er as mad i' o mi life,
Cleautin' th' kids an' cursin' th' wife,
Awm sure mi brains han left mi yed,
Ther's nowt to do but goh toh bed,
At six o'clock o' th' Setturdy neet,
They're o i' bed i' eawr street,
When Owdham's lost.

AMMON WRIGLEY

from Rites

Look wha' happen las' week at de O-
val!

At de Oval?
Wha' happen las' week at de Oval?

You mean to say that you come
in here wid dat lime-skin cone

that you callin' a hat
pun you head, an' them slip slop shoe strap

on to you foot like a touris';
you sprawl you ass

all over my chair widdout ask-
in' me please leave nor licence,

wastin' muh time when you know very well that
    uh cahn fine
enough to finish these zoot suits

'fore Christmas; an' on top
o' all this, you could wine up de nerve to stop

me cool cool cool in de middle
o' all me needle

an' t'read; make me prick me hand im me haste;
an' tell me broad an' bole to me face

THAT YOU DOAN REALLY KNOW WHA'
    HAPPEN
At Kensington Oval?

We was *only* playin' de MCC, man;
M—C—C
who come all de way out from Inglan.

We was battin', you see;
score wasn't too bad; one
hurren an' ninety-

seven fuh three.
The openers out, Tae Worrell out,
Everton Weekes jus' glide two fuh fifty

an' jack, is de GIANT to come!
Feller name Wardle
was bowlin'; tossin' it up

sweet sweet slow-medium syrup.
Firs' ball . . .
'N . . . o . . . o . . .'

back down de wicket to Wardle.
Secon' ball . . .
'N . . . o . . . o . . .'

Back down de wicket to Wardle.
Third ball comin' up
an' we know wha' goin' happen to syrup:

Clyde back pun he back
foot an' *prax*!
is through extra cover an' four red runs all de
    way.

'You see dat shot?' The people was shoutin';
'Jesus Chrise, Man, wunna see dat shot?'
All over de groun' fellers shakin' hands wid each
    other

as if was *they* wheelin' de willow
as if was *them* had the power;
one man run out pun de field wid a red fowl cock

goin' quawk quawk quawk in 'e han';
would 'a give it to Clyde right then an' right
    there
if a police hadn't stop 'e!

An' in front o' where I was sittin',
one ball-headed sceptic snatch hat off he head
as if he did crazy

EDWARD KAMAU BRATHWAITE

High Talk

Processions that lack high stilts have nothing that
    catches the eye.
What if my great-grandad had a pair that were
    twenty foot high,
And mine were but fifteen foot, no modern stalks
    upon higher,
Some rogue of the world stole them to patch up a
    fence or a fire.
Because piebald ponies, led bears, caged lions,
    make but poor shows,
Because children demand Daddy-long-legs upon
    his timber toes,
Because women in the upper storeys demand a
    face at the pane,
That patching old heels they may shriek, I take to
    chisel and plane.

Malachi Stilt-Jack am I, whatever I learned has
    run wild.
From collar to collar, from stilt to stilt, from
    father to child.
All metaphor, Malachi, stilts and all. A barnacle
    goose
Far up in the stretches of night; night splits and
    the dawn breaks loose;
I, through the terrible novelty of light, stalk on,
    stalk on;
Those great sea-horses bare their teeth and laugh
    at the dawn.

W. B. YEATS

Whip-the-World

Mountains and seas
whirl   Birl under his wings
twist   Till a' gaes in a kink
shimmering   O' skimmerin' rings.

He lays on wi' his sang,
willing   The wullie wee chap,
makes   Till he gars earth bizz
spinning top   Like a dozened tap.

to one side   Syne he hings sidelins
Watchin' hoo lang
It tak's till it staggers
Oot o' his sang.

Aye it tak's langer
And ane o' thae days
'I'll thraw't in a whirl
It'll bide in,' he says.

HUGH MACDIARMID

The Wind, the Clock, the We

The wind has at last got into the clock –
Every minute for itself.
There's no more sixty,
There's no more twelve,
It's as late as it's early.

The rain has washed out the numbers.
The trees don't care what happens.
Time has become a landscape
Of suicidal leaves and stoic branches –
Unpainted as fast as painted.
Or perhaps that's too much to say,
With the clock devouring itself
And the minutes given leave to die.

The sea's no picture at all.
To sea, then: that's time now,
And every mortal heart's a sailor
Sworn to vengeance on the wind,
To hurl life back into the thin teeth
Out of which first it whistled,
An idiotic defiance of it knew not what
Screeching round the studying clock.

Now there's neither ticking nor blowing.
The ship has gone down with its men,
The sea with the ship, the wind with the sea.
The wind at last got into the clock,
The clock at last got into the wind,
The world at last got out of itself.

At last we can make sense, you and I,
You lone survivors on paper,
The wind's boldness and the clock's care
Become a voiceless language,
And I the story hushed in it –
Is more to say of me?
Do I say more than self-choked falsity
Can repeat word for word after me,
The script not altered by a breath
Of perhaps meaning otherwise?

LAURA RIDING

from Song of Myself

I celebrate myself, and sing myself,
And what I assume you shall assume,
For every atom belonging to me as good belongs
   to you.

I loafe and invite my soul,
I lean and loafe at my ease observing a spear of
   summer grass.

My tongue, every atom of my blood, form'd
    from this soil, this air,
Born here of parents born here from parents the
    same, and their parents the same,
I, now thirty-seven years old in perfect health
    begin,
Hoping to cease not till death.

Creeds and schools in abeyance,
Retiring back a while sufficed at what they are,
    but never forgotten,
I harbor for good or bad, I permit to speak at
    every hazard,
Nature without check with original energy.

Houses and rooms are full of perfumes, the
    shelves are crowded with perfumes,
I breathe the fragrance myself and know it and
    like it,
The distillation would intoxicate me also, but I
    shall not let it.

The atmosphere is not a perfume, it has no taste
    of the distillation, it is odorless,
It is for my mouth forever, I am in love with it,
I will go to the bank by the wood and become
    undisguised and naked,
I am mad for it to be in contact with me.
The smoke of my own breath,
Echoes, ripples, buzz'd whispers, love-root, silk-
    thread, crotch and vine,
My respiration and inspiration, the beating of my
    heart, the passing of blood and air through my
    lungs,
The sniff of green leaves and dry leaves, and of
    the shore and dark-color'd sea-rocks, and of
    hay in the barn,

The sound of the belch'd words of my voice
    loos'd to the eddies of the wind,
A few light kisses, a few embraces, a reaching
    around of arms,
The play of shine and shade on the trees as the
    supple boughs wag,
The delight alone or in the rush of the streets, or
    along the fields and hill-sides,
The feeling of health, the full-noon trill, the song
    of me rising from bed and meeting the sun.

Have you reckon'd a thousand acres much? have
    you reckon'd the earth much?
Have you practis'd so long to learn to read?
Have you felt so proud to get at the meaning of
    poems?

Stop this day and night with me and you shall
    possess the origin of all poems,
You shall possess the good of the earth and sun,
    (there are millions of suns left,)
You shall no longer take things at second or
    third hand, nor look through the eyes of the
    dead, nor feed on the spectres in books,
You shall not look through my eyes either, nor
    take things from me,
You shall listen to all sides and filter them from
    your self.

I have heard what the talkers were talking, the
    talk of the beginning and the end,
But I do not talk of the beginning or the end.

There was never any more inception than there is
  now,
Nor any more youth or age than there is now,
And will never be any more perfection than there
  is now,
Nor any more heaven or hell than there is now.

Urge and urge and urge,
Always the procreant urge of the world.

Out of the dimness opposite equals advance,
  always substance and increase, always sex,
Always a knit of identity, always distinction,
  always a breed of life.

To elaborate is no avail, learn'd and unlearn'd
  feel that it is so.

Sure as the most certain sure, plumb in the
  uprights, well entretied, braced in the beams,
Stout as a horse, affectionate, haughty, electrical,
I and this mystery here we stand.

Clear and sweet is my soul, and clear and sweet
  is all that is not my soul.

Lack one lacks both, and the unseen is proved by
  the seen,
Till that becomes unseen and receives proof in its
  turn.

Showing the best and dividing it from the worst
  age vexes age,
Knowing the perfect fitness and equanimity of
  things, while they discuss I am silent, and go
  bathe and admire myself.

Welcome is every organ and attribute of me, and
    of any man hearty and clean,
Not an inch nor a particle of an inch is vile, and
    none shall be less familiar than the rest.

I am satisfied — I see, dance, laugh, sing;
As the hugging and loving bed-fellow sleeps at
    my side through the night, and withdraws at
    the peep of the day with stealthy tread,
Leaving me baskets cover'd with white towels
    swelling the house with their plenty,
Shall I postpone my acceptation and realization
    and scream at my eyes,
That they turn from gazing after and down the
    road,
And forthwith cipher and show me to a cent,
Exactly the value of one and exactly the value of
    two, and which is ahead?

Trippers and askers surround me,
People I meet, the effect upon me of my early life
    or the ward and city I live in, or the nation,
The latest dates, discoveries, inventions, societies,
    authors old and new,
My dinner, dress, associates, looks, compliments,
    dues,
The real or fancied indifference of some man or
    woman I love,
The sickness of one of my folks or of myself, or
    ill-doing or loss or lack of money, or
    depressions or exaltations,
Battles, the horrors of fratricidal war, the fever of
    doubtful news, the fitful events;
These come to me days and nights and go from
    me again,
But they are not the Me myself.

Apart from the pulling and hauling stands what I
    am,
Stands amused, complacent, compassionating,
    idle, unitary,
Looks down, is erect, or bends an arm on an
    impalpable certain rest,
Looking with side-curved head curious what will
    come next,
Both in and out of the game and watching and
    wondering at it.

Backward I see in my own days where I sweated
    through fog with linguists and contenders,
I have no mockings or arguments, I witness and
    wait.

I believe in you my soul, the other I am must not
    abase itself to you,
And you must not be abased to the other.

Loafe with me on the grass, loose the stop from
    your throat,
Not words, not music or rhyme I want, not
    custom or lecture, not even the best,
Only the lull I like, the hum of your valvèd voice.

I mind how once we lay such a transparent
    summer morning,
How you settled your head athwart my hips and
    gently turn'd over upon me,
And parted the shirt from my bosom-bone, and
    plunged your tongue to my bare-stript heart,
And reach'd till you felt my beard, and reach'd
    till you held my feet.

Swiftly arose and spread around me the peace
  and knowledge that pass all the argument of
  the earth,
And I know that the hand of God is the promise
  of my own,
And I know that the spirit of God is the brother
  of my own,
And that all the men ever born are also my
  brothers, and the women my sisters and lovers,
And that a kelson of the creation is love,
And limitless are leaves stiff or drooping in the
  fields,
And brown ants in the little wells beneath them,
And mossy scabs of the worm fence, heap'd
  stones, elder, mullein and poke-weed.

A child said *What is the grass?* fetching it to me
  with full hands;
How could I answer the child? I do not know
  what it is any more than he.

I guess it must be the flag of my disposition, out
  of hopeful green stuff woven.

Or I guess it is the handkerchief of the Lord,
A scented gift and the remembrancer designedly
  dropt,
Bearing the owner's name someway in the
  corners, that we may see and remark, and say
  Whose?

Or I guess the grass is itself a child, the produced
  babe of the vegetation.

Or I guess it is a uniform hieroglyphic,
And it means, Sprouting alike in broad zones and
    narrow zones,
Growing among black folks as among white,
Kanuck, Tuckahoe, Congressman, Cuff, I give
    them the same, I receive them the same.

And now it seems to me the beautiful uncut hair
    of graves.

Tenderly will I use you curling grass,
It may be you transpire from the breasts of
    young men,
It may be if I had known them I would have
    loved them,
It may be you are from old people, or from
    offspring taken soon out of their mothers' laps,
And here you are the mothers' laps.

This grass is very dark to be from the white
    heads of old mothers,
Darker than the colorless beards of old men,
Dark to come from under the faint red roofs of
    mouths.

O I perceive after all so many uttering tongues,
And I perceive they do not come from the roofs
    of mouths for nothing.
I wish I could translate the hints about the dead
    young men and women,
And the hints about old men and mothers, and
    the offspring taken soon out of their laps.

What do you think has become of the young and
    old men?
And what do you think has become of the
    women and children?

They are alive and well somewhere,
The smallest sprout shows there is really no death,
And if ever there was it led forward life, and does
    not wait at the end to arrest it,
And ceas'd the moment life appear'd.

All goes onward and outward, nothing collapses,
And to die is different from what any one
    supposed, and luckier.

Has any one supposed it lucky to be born?
I hasten to inform him or her it is just as lucky to
    die, and I know it.

I pass death with the dying and birth with the
    new-wash'd babe, and am not contain'd
    between my hat and boots,
And peruse manifold objects, no two alike and
    every one good,
The earth good and the stars good, and their
    adjuncts all good.

I am not an earth nor an adjunct of an earth,
I am the mate and companion of people, all just
    as immortal and fathomless as myself,
(They do not know how immortal, but I know.)

Every kind for itself and its own, for me mine
    male and female,
For me those that have been boys and that love
    women,
For me the man that is proud and feels how it
    stings to be slighted,
For me the sweet-heart and the old maid, for me
    mothers and the mothers of mothers,
For me lips that have smiled, eyes that have shed
    tears,
For me children and the begetters of children.

Undrape! you are not guilty to me nor stale nor
     discarded,
I see through the broadcloth and gingham
     whether or no,
And am around, tenacious, acquisitive, tireless,
     and cannot be shaken away.

The little one sleeps in its cradle,
I lift the gauze and look a long time, and silently
     brush away flies with my hand.

The youngster and the red-faced girl turn aside
     up the bushy hill,
I peeringly view them from the top.

The suicide sprawls on the bloody floor of the
     bedroom,
I witness the corpse with its dabbled hair, I note
     where the pistol has fallen.

The blab of the pave, tires of carts, sluff of boot-
     soles, talk of the promenaders,
The heavy omnibus, the driver with his
     interrogating thumb, the clank of the shod
     horses on the granite floor,
The snow-sleighs, clinking, shouted jokes, pelts
     of snow-balls,
The hurrahs for popular favorites, the fury of
     rous'd mobs,
The flap of the curtain'd litter, a sick man inside
     borne to the hospital,
The meeting of enemies, the sudden oath, the
     blows and fall,

The excited crowd, the policeman with his star
    quickly working his passage to the centre of
    the crowd,
The impassive stones that receive and return so
    many echoes,
What groans of over-fed or half-starv'd who fall
    sunstruck or in fits,
What exclamations of women taken suddenly
    who hurry home and give birth to babes,
What living and buried speech is always vibrating
    here, what howls restrain'd by decorum,
Arrests of criminals, slights, adulterous offers
    made, acceptances, rejections with convex lips,
I mind them or the show or resonance of them —
    I come and I depart.

The big doors of the country barn stand open
    and ready,
The dried grass of the harvest-time loads the
    slow-drawn wagon,
The clear light plays on the brown gray and
    green intertinged,
The armfuls are pack'd to the sagging mow.

I am there, I help, I came stretch'd atop of the
    load,
I felt its soft jolts, one leg reclined on the other,
I jump from the cross-beams and seize the clover
    and timothy,
And roll head over heels and tangle my hair full
    of wisps.

Alone far in the wilds and mountains I hunt,
Wandering amazed at my own lightness and glee,
In the late afternoon choosing a safe spot to pass
    the night,
Kindling a fire and broiling the fresh-kill'd game,
Falling asleep on the gather'd leaves with my dog
    and gun by my side.

The Yankee clipper is under her sky-sails, she
    cuts the sparkle and scud,
My eyes settle the land, I bend at her prow or
    shout joyously from the deck.

The boatmen and clam-diggers arose early and
    stopt for me,
I tuck'd my trowser-ends in my boots and went
    and had a good time;
You should have been with us that day round the
    chowder-kettle.

I saw the marriage of the trapper in the open air
    in the far west, the bride was a red girl,
Her father and his friends sat near cross-legged
    and dumbly smoking, they had moccasins to
    their feet and large thick blankets hanging
    from their shoulders,
On a bank lounged the trapper, he was drest
    mostly in skins, his luxuriant beard and curls
    protected his neck, he held his bride by the
    hand,
She had long eyelashes, her head was bare, her
    coarse straight locks descended upon her
    voluptuous limbs and reach'd to her feet.

The runaway slave came to my house and stopt
  outside,
I heard his motions crackling the twigs of the
  woodpile,
Through the swung half-door of the kitchen I
  saw him limpsy and weak,
And went where he sat on a log and led him in
  and assured him,
And brought water and fill'd a tub for his
  sweated body and bruis'd feet,
And gave him a room that enter'd from my own,
  and gave him some coarse clean clothes,
And remember perfectly well his revolving eyes
  and his awkwardness,
And remember putting plasters on the galls of his
  neck and ankles;
He staid with me a week before he was
  recuperated and pass'd north,
I had him sit next me at table, my fire-lock lean'd
  in the corner.

. . . .

Stretch'd and still lies the midnight,
Two great bulls motionless on the breast of the
  darkness,
Our vessel riddled and slowly sinking,
  preparations to pass to the one we have
  conquer'd,
The captain on the quarter-deck coldly giving his
  orders through a countenance white as a sheet,
Near by the corpse of the child that serv'd in the
  cabin,
The dead face of an old salt with long white hair
  and carefully curl'd whiskers,
The flames spite of all that can be done flickering
  aloft and below,

The husky voices of the two or three officers yet
   fit for duty,
Formless stacks of bodies and bodies by
   themselves, dabs of flesh upon the masts and
   spars,
Cut of cordage, dangle of rigging, slight shock of
   the soothe of waves,
Black and impassive guns, litter of powder-
   parcels, strong scent,
A few large stars overhead, silent and mournful
   shining,
Delicate sniffs of sea-breeze, smells of sedgy grass
   and fields by the shore, death-messages given
   in charge to survivors,
The hiss of the surgeon's knife, the gnawing teeth
   of his saw,
Wheeze, cluck, swash of falling blood, short wild
   scream, and long, dull, tapering groan,
These so, these irretrievable.

There is that in me – I do not know what it is –
   but I know it is in me.

Wrench'd and sweaty – calm and cool then my
   body becomes,
I sleep – I sleep long.

I do not know it – it is without name – it is a
   word unsaid,
It is not in any dictionary, utterance, symbol.

Something it swings on more than the earth I
   swing on,
To it the creation is the friend whose embracing
   awakes me.

Perhaps I might tell more. Outlines! I plead for
    my brothers and sisters.

Do you see O my brothers and sisters?
It is not chaos or death – it is form, union, plan –
    it is eternal life – it is Happiness.

The past and present wilt – I have fill'd them,
    emptied them,
And proceed to fill my next fold of the future.

Listener up there! what have you to confide to
    me?
Look in my face while I snuff the sidle of
    evening,
(Talk honestly, no one else hears you, and I stay
    only a minute longer.)

Do I contradict myself?
Very well then I contradict myself,
(I am large, I contain multitudes.)

I concentrate toward them that are nigh, I wait
    on the doorslab.
Who has done his day's work? who will soonest
    be through with his supper?
Who wishes to walk with me?

Will you speak before I am gone? will you prove
    already too late?

The spotted hawk swoops by and accuses me, he
    complains of my gab and my loitering.

I too am not a bit tamed, I too am
    untranslatable,
I sound my barbaric yawp over the roofs of the
    world.

The last scud of day holds back for me,
It flings my likeness after the rest and true as any
    on the shadow'd wilds,
It coaxes me to the vapor and the dusk.

I depart as air, I shake my white locks at the
    runaway sun,
I effuse my flesh in eddies, and drift it in lacy
    jags.

I bequeath myself to the dirt to grow from the
    grass I love,
If you want me again look for me under your
    boot-soles.

You will hardly know who I am or what I mean,
But I shall be good health to you nevertheless,
And filter and fibre your blood.

Failing to fetch me at first keep encouraged,
Missing me one place search another,
I stop somewhere waiting for you.

WALT WHITMAN

Convicts' Rum Song

Cut yer name across me backbone
stretch me skin across a drum
iron me up on Pinchgut Island
from today till Kingdom Come!

I will eat yer Norfolk dumpling
like a juicy Spanish plum
even dance the Newgate Hornpipe
if ye'll only gimme RUM!

ANON

'Spende and god schall sende'

Spende and god schall sende
evermore spare and ermor care
non peni   non ware
non catel   non care
   go peni go

ANON

Complaints

The Magryme

headache

My heid did yak yester nicht
this day to mak that I na micht
so sair the magryme dois me menzie
perseing my brow as ony ganzie
that scant I luik may on the licht

and now Schir laitlie eftir mes
to dyt thocht I begowthe to dres   prepare
the sentence lay full evill till find
unsleipit in my heid behind
dullit in dulnes and distres

full oft at morrow I upryse
quhen that my curage sleipeing lyis
for mirth for menstrallie and play
for din nor danceing nor deray
it will nocht walkin me no wise

WILLIAM DUNBAR

headache

write poetry
disable
arrow

the King/mass
write/however/began/
difficult
not having slept/memory

desire

revelry
awaken

Soliloquy of the Spanish Cloister

I

Gr-r-r – there go, my heart's abhorrence!
  Water your damned flower-pots, do!
If hate killed men, Brother Lawrence,
  God's blood, would not mine kill you!
What? your myrtle-bush wants trimming?
  Oh, that rose has prior claims –
Needs its leaden vase filled brimming?
  Hell dry you up with its flames!

II

At the meal we sit together:
   Salve tibi! I must hear
Wise talk of the kind of weather,
   Sort of season, time of year:
Not a plenteous cork-crop: scarcely
   Dare we hope oak-galls, I doubt:
What's the Latin name for 'parsley'?
   What's the Greek name for Swine's Snout?

III

Whew! We'll have our platter burnished,
   Laid with care on our own shelf!
With a fire-new spoon we're furnished,
   And a goblet for ourself,
Rinsed like something sacrificial
   Ere 't is fit to touch our chaps –
Marked with L. for our initial!
   (He-he! There his lily snaps!)

IV

Saint, forsooth! While brown Dolores
   Squats outside the Convent bank
With Sanchicha, telling stories,
   Steeping tresses in the tank,
Blue-black, lustrous, thick like horsehairs,
   – Can't I see his dead eye glow,
Bright as 't were a Barbary corsair's?
   (That is, if he'd let it show!)

V

When he finishes refection,
    Knife and fork he never lays
Cross-wise, to my recollection,
    As do I, in Jesu's praise.
I the Trinity illustrate,
    Drinking watered orange-pulp –
In three sips the Arian frustrate;
    While he drains his at one gulp.

VI

Oh, those melons? If he's able
    We're to have a feast! so nice!
One goes to the Abbot's table,
    All of us get each a slice.
How go on your flowers? None double?
    Not one fruit-sort can you spy?
Strange! – And I, too, at such trouble,
    Keep them close-nipped on the sly!

VII

There's a great text in Galatians,
    Once you trip on it, entails
Twenty-nine distinct damnations,
    One sure, if another fails:
If I trip him just a-dying,
    Sure of heaven as sure can be,
Spin him round and send him flying
    Off to hell, a Manichee?

VIII

Or, my scrofulous French novel
  On grey paper with blunt type!
Simply glance at it, you grovel
  Hand and foot in Belial's gripe:
If I double down its pages
  At the woeful sixteeenth print,
When he gathers his greengages,
  Ope a sieve and slip it in 't?

IX

Or, there's Satan! – one might venture
  Pledge one's soul to him, yet leave
Such a flaw in the indenture
  As he'd miss till, past retrieve,
Blasted lay that rose-acacia
  We're so proud of! *Hy, Zy, Hine* . . .
'St, there's Vespers! *Plena gratiâ
  Ave, Virgo!* Gr-r-r – you swine!

ROBERT BROWNING

from Amours de Voyage, I

Claude to Eustace

Luther, they say, was unwise; he didn't see how
    things were going;
Luther was foolish, – but, O great God! what
    call you Ignatius?
O my tolerant soul, be still! but you talk of
    barbarians,
Alaric, Attila, Genseric; – why, they came, they
    killed, they
Ravaged, and went on their way; but these vile,
    tyrannous Spaniards,
These are here still, – how long, O ye Heavens,
    in the country of Dante?

These, that fanaticized Europe, which now can
    forget them, release not
This, their choicest of prey, this Italy; here you
    see them, –
Here, with emasculate pupils and gimcrack
    churches of Gesu,
Pseudo-learning and lies, confessional-boxes and
    postures, –
Here, with metallic beliefs and regimental
    devotions, –
Here, overcrusting with slime, perverting,
    defacing, debasing,
Michel Angelo's dome, that had hung the
    Pantheon in heaven,
Raphael's Joys and Graces, and thy clear stars,
    Galileo!

ARTHUR HUGH CLOUGH

'They shut me up in Prose'

They shut me up in Prose –
As when a little Girl
They put me in the Closet –
Because they liked me 'still' –

Still! Could themself have peeped –
And seen my Brain – go round –
They might as wise have lodged a Bird
For Treason – in the Pound –

Himself has but to will
And easy as a Star
Abolish his Captivity –
And laugh – No more have I –

EMILY DICKINSON

Lucy's Letter

Things harness me here. I long
have a yarn   for we labrish bad. Doors
not fixed open here.
No Leela either. No Cousin
Lil, Miss Lottie or Bro'-Uncle.
dawn   Dayclean doesn't have cockcrowin'.
Midmornin' doesn' bring
Caribbean fruit   Cousin-Maa with her naseberry tray.
Afternoon doesn' give a ragged
Manwell, strung with fish
like bright leaves. Seven days
play same note in London, chile.
But Leela, money-rustle regular.

Me dear, I don' laugh now,
not'n' like we thunder claps
in darkness on verandah.
I turn a battery hen
in 'lectric light, day an' night.
No mood can touch one
mango season back at Yard.
At least though I did start
evening school once.
An' doctors free, chile.

London isn't like we
village dirt road, you know
Leela: it a parish
of a pasture-lan' what
grown crisscross streets,
an' they lie down to my door.
But I lock myself in.
I carry keys everywhere.
Life here's no open summer,
girl. But Sat'day mornin' don'
find me han' dry, don' find me face
a heavy cloud over the man.

An' though he still have
a weekend mind for bat'n'ball
he wash a dirty dish now, me dear.
It sweet him I on the Pill.

We get money for holidays.
But there's no sun-hot
to enjoy cool breeze.

Leela, I really a sponge
you know, for traffic noise,
for work noise, for halfway
intentions, for halfway smiles,
for clockwatching' an' col' weather.
I hope you don' think I gone
too fat when we meet.
I booked up to come an' soak
the children in daylight.

JAMES BERRY

The Author's Quietus

Address'd to his Dear Friend, Jemmy Worsdale

This itch of scribbling has no end, no ease,
Damn'd if you fail, and envy'd if you please;
Uncertain pleasure for most certain pain:
Well, Solomon says right, All things are vain;
'Tis better that a man should eat and drink.
Here! – Take away this ugly pen and ink!
Come, James! – let's have a bottle and a bit;
There's something solid in that kind of wit.

HENRY CAREY

Exeunt Omnes

I

Everybody else, then, going,
And I still left where the fair was? . . .
Much have I seen of neighbour loungers
Making a lusty showing,
Each now past all knowing.

II

There is an air of blankness
In the street and the littered spaces;
Thoroughfare, steeple, bridge and highway
Wizen themselves to lankness;
Kennels dribble dankness.

III
Folk all fade. And whither,
As I wait alone where the fair was?
Into the clammy and numbing night-fog
    Whence they entered hither.
    Soon one more goes thither!

THOMAS HARDY

The Greenhouse Vanity

Sea-perch over paddocks. Dunes. Salt light
    everywhere low down
just like the increasing gleam between Bass Strait
    islands
nine thousand years ago. In an offshore tidal
    town
the Folk Museum moans of a stormy night, and
    shrills:

You made the oceans rise! Rubbish, it was you!
The Pioneers Room and Recent Times are
    quarrelling.
By day the flannelled drone: up at daylight, lard
    and tea,
axe and crosscut till black dark, once I shot a
    ding-

o at the cradle, there at fifteen, the only white
    woman
ploughing by hand, parrot pie, we sewed our
    own music –
Recent Times blink and hum; one bends to B-cup
    a pair,
each point the rouge inside a kiss; one boosts the
    tape-deck

till coal conveyors rattle and mile-high
    smokestacks pant
Beige! beige! on every viewscreen. This should re-
    float your Hardships,
despoiler, black-shooter! – Nature's caught up
    with you, Trendywank! –
So. We changed the weather. – Yep. Humans.
    We made and unmade the maps.

LES MURRAY

Nonsence

Like to the thund'ring tone of unspoke speeches,
Or like a lobster clad in logick breeches,
Or like the gray freeze of a crimson cat,
Or like a moon-calf in a slipsho hat,
Or like a shadow when the sunne is gone,
Or like a thought that neere was thought upon,
    Even such is man, who never was begoten
    Untill his children were both dead and rotten.

Like to the fiery touchstone of a cabbage,
Or like a crablouse with his bagge and baggage,
Or like th'abortive issue of a fizle,
Or like the bagge-pudding of a plowmans
    whistle,
Or like the foure square circle of a ring,
Or like the singing of hey down a ding,
    Even such is man, who, breathles without
    doubt,
    Spake to smal purpose when his tongue was
    out.

Like to the greene fresh fading withered rose,
Or like to rime or verse that runs in prose,
Or like the humbles of a tinder-box,
Or like a man that's sound, yet hath the poxe,
Or like a hobnaile coyn'd in single pence,
Or like the present preterperfect tense,
   Even such is man, who dy'd and then did laffe
   To see such strange lines writ on's Epitaph.

RICHARD CORBETT

Graffiti

Belfast Graffiti

GIVE THEM THEIR RIGHTS – NOT THEIR LAST RITES

ONE   ONE
FAITH   CROWN

WHEN YOU CAME TO THIS LAND
YOU SAID YOU CAME TO UNDERSTAND
SOLDIER WE'RE TIRED OF YOUR UNDERSTAND-
ING TIRED OF BRITISH TROOPS ON OUR SOIL
TIRED OF THE KNOCK UPON THE DOOR
TIRED OF THE RIFLE-BUTT ON THE HEAD
TIRED OF THE JAILS' AND THE BEATINGS
TIRED OF THE DEATHS OF OLD FRIENDS
TIRED OF THE TEARS AND FUNERALS.
IS THIS YOUR UNDERSTANDING?

WE SHALL NOT EXCHANGE THE BLUE SKIES OF
    FREEDOM
FOR THE GREY SKIES OF AN IRISH REPUBLIC

GILMORE WILL BE GOT SOONER OR LATER

WHEN THOSE WHO MAKE THE LAW BREAK THE LAW IN
   THE NAME OF THE LAW THERE IS NO LAW

IS THERE LIFE BEFORE DEATH?

Subway Art

THERE WAS ONCE A TIME
WHEN THE LEXINGTON WAS A BEAUTIFUL LINE
WHEN THE CHILDREN OF THE GHETTO EXPRESSED
WITH ART, NOT WITH CRIME. BUT THEN AS
EVOLUTION PAST, THE TRANSITS BUFFING DID ITS
BLAST. AND NOW THE TRAINS LOOK LIKE RUSTED
TRASH. NOW WE WONDER IF GRAFFITI WILL
EVER LAST . . . ????????

Don't spray it say it

A little coitus
Never hoitus

The Realm of You

Fair Rosa

Fair Rosa was a lovely child
a lovely child   a lovely child
fair Rosa was a lovely child
a long time ago

a wicked fairy cast a spell
cast a spell   cast a spell
a wicked fairy cast a spell
a long time ago

fair Rosa slept for a hundred years
a hundred years   a hundred years
fair Rosa slept for a hundred years
a long time ago

the hedges they all grew around
grew around   grew around
the hedges they all grew around
a long time ago

a handsome prince came ariding by
riding by   riding by
a handsome prince came ariding by
a long time ago

he cut the hedges one by one
one by one   one by one
he cut the hedges one by one
a long time ago

he kissed fair Rosa's lilywhite hand
lilywhite hand   lilywhite hand
he kissed fair Rosa's lilywhite hand
a long time ago

fair Rosa will not sleep no more
sleep no more   sleep no more
fair Rosa will not sleep no more
a long time ago

ANON

Dunt Dunt Dunt Pittie Pattie

On Whitsunday morning
I went to the fair
my yellowhaird laddie
was selling his ware
he gied me sic a blythe blink
with his bonny black ee
and a dear blink and a fair blink
it was unto me

I wist not what ailed me
when my laddie cam in
the little wee sternies
flew aye frae my een
and the sweat it dropped down
from my very ee bree
for my heart aye played
dunt dunt dunt pittie pattie

I wist not what ailed me
when I went to my bed
I tossd and I tumbled
and sleep frae me fled
now its sleeping and waking
he's aye in my ee
and my heart aye plays
dunt dunt dunt pittie pattie

ANON

pupils

'It's like the Light'

It's like the Light –
A fashionless Delight –
It's like the Bee –
A dateless – Melody –

It's like the Woods –
Private – Like the Breeze –
Phraseless – yet it stirs
The proudest Trees –

It's like the Morning –
Best – when it's done –
And the Everlasting Clocks –
Chime – Noon!

EMILY DICKINSON

Chapmen

pedlars	We ben chapmen lyght of fote
	the fowle weyis for to fle
carry	we bern abowtyn non cattes skynnys
	pursis perlis sylver pynnis
veils	smale wympeles for ladyis chynnys
buy	damsele bey sum ware of me
nonce	I have a poket for the nonys
two	therine ben tweyne precyous stonys
tried them once	damsele hadde ye asayid hem onys
	ye shuld the rathere gon with me

jelly/gift
feet
strike/has
guess

I have a jelyf of Godes sonde
withoutyn fyt it can stonde
it can smytyn and haght non honde
ryd yourself quat it may be

I have a powder for to selle
quat it is can I not telle
it makit maydenys wombys to swelle
therof I have a quantyte

ANON

'Come slowly – Eden!'

Come slowly – Eden!
Lips unused to Thee –
Bashful – sip thy Jessamines –
As the fainting Bee –

Reaching late his flower,
Round her chamber hums –
Counts his nectars –
Enters – and is lost in Balms.

EMILY DICKINSON

'Did the Harebell loose her girdle'

Did the Harebell loose her girdle
To the lover Bee
Would the Bee the Harebell *hallow*
Much as formerly?

Did the 'Paradise' – persuaded –
Yield her moat of pearl –
Would the Eden *be* an Eden,
Or the Earl – an *Earl*?

EMILY DICKINSON

Green Gravel

Green gravel   green gravel
your grass is so green
you're the fairest young damsel
I ever have seen

I washed her   I dressed her
I clothed her in silk
and I wrote down her name
with a glass pen and ink

O Kathleen   O Kathleen
your true love is dead
I sent you a letter
to turn back your head

ANON

Morant Bay

Me go to Morant Bay

cheap cloth · bahlimbo

me see wun coolie gal

bahlimbo

lord me love the gal

bahlimbo

me tell her wait fe me

bahlimbo

the gal no wait at all

bahlimbo

me ride me ride me ride

bahlimbo

me catch her on the way

bahlimbo

kiss me bahss her all the way

bahlimbo

the mumma say me rude

bahlimbo

but that no rude at all

bahlimbo

for woman cloth so cheap

bahlimbo

twopence two yard fe bit

bahlimbo

man cloth so dear

bahlimbo

wun poun a yard

bahlimbo

ANON

Meeting at Night

I

The grey sea and the long black land;
And the yellow half-moon large and low;
And the startled little waves that leap
In fiery ringlets from their sleep,
As I gain the cove with pushing prow,
And quench its speed i' the slushy sand.

II

Then a mile of warm sea-scented beach;
Three fields to cross till a farm appears;
A tap at the pane, the quick sharp scratch
And blue spurt of a lighted match,
And a voice less loud, thro' its joys and fears,
Than the two hearts beating each to each!

ROBERT BROWNING

Wasting Time

Nooo!
me nah call him
maybe me should?
no sah!
mek him guh tink me
a court him.

Cho!
but me would a like
fi call him.
but him a guh tink
me a run him down.

No sah!
go along   mek him galang.

But cho!
wha it matta
wha him tink.
Me nah run him down.
so might as cheap me call
him.

Cho!
all those men want   dem yah man wan
women to chase them   oman call call dem.
den dem tun roun
tek vantage.
but wha me care
dem tek vantage anyway.

Cho!
me nah call him.
maybe me should?

no sah!
me nah call nuh man
fi him come breathe
hot air pon me chest
den tun round
tek vantage.

but me should a
call him yuh know.

but tap! why him
kyaan call tu.

Cho!
a wonda
should me call him though?

(silence, silence, silence)

howdy do man.

(hesitation, hesitation, hesitation)
I would like fi
speak to
(pause, pause, pause)

I would like fi
speak to Missa . . .

OPAL PALMER

Song

Whenas the rye reach to the chin,
And chopcherry, chopcherry ripe within,
Strawberries swimming in the cream,
And schoolboys playing in the stream;
Then oh, then oh, then oh, my true Love said,
Till that time come again
She could not live a maid.

GEORGE PEELE

The Drained Cup

T' snow is witherin' off'n th' gress –
        Lad, should I tell thee summat?
T' snow is witherin' off'n th' gress
An' mist is suckin' at th' spots o' snow,
An' ower a' the thaw an' mess
There's a moon, full blow.
        Lad, but I'm tellin' thee summat!

Tha's bin snowed up i' this cottage wi' me —
    'Ark, tha'rt for hearin' summat!
Tha's bin snowed up i' this cottage wi' me
While t' clocks 'as a' run down an' stopped,
An' t' short days goin' unknown ter thee
Unbeknown has dropped.
    Yi, but I'm tellin' thee summat.

How many days dost think has gone?
    Now, lad, I'm axin' thee summat.
How many days dost think has gone?
How many times has t' candle-light shone
On thy face as tha got more white an' wan?
   — Seven days, my lad, or none!
    Aren't ter hearin' summat?

Tha come ter say good-bye ter me,
    Tha wert frit o' summat.
Tha come ter ha' finished an' done wi' me
An' off to a gel as wor younger than me,
An' fresh an' more nicer for marryin' wi' —
    Yi, but tha'rt frit o' summat.

Ah wunna kiss thee, tha trembles so!
    Tha'rt daunted, or summat.
frightened   Tha arena very flig ter go.
Dost want me ter want thee again? Nay though,
There's hardly owt left o' thee; get up an' go!
    Or dear o' me, say summat.

Tha wanted ter leave me that bad, tha knows!
    Doesn't ter know it?
But tha wanted me more ter want thee, so's
Tha could let thy very soul out. A man
Like thee can't rest till his last spunk goes
Out of 'im into a woman as can
    Draw it out of 'im. Did ter know it?

Tha thought tha wanted a little wench,
    Ay, lad, I'll tell thee thy mind.
Tha thought tha wanted a little wench
As 'ud make thee a wife an' look up ter thee.
As 'ud wince when that touched 'er close, an'
   blench
An' lie frightened ter death under thee.
    She worn't hard ter find.

Tha thought tha wanted to be rid o' me.
    'Appen tha did, an' a'.
Tha thought tha wanted ter marry an' see
If ter couldna be master an' th' woman's boss.
Tha'd need a woman different from me,
An' tha knowed it; ay, yet tha comes across
    Ter say good-bye! an' a'.

I tell thee tha won't be satisfied,
    Tha might as well listen, tha knows.
I tell thee tha won't be satisfied
Till a woman has drawn the last last drop
O' thy spunk, an' tha'rt empty an' mortified.
Empty an' empty from bottom to top.
    It's true, tha knows.

Tha'rt one o' th' men as has got to drain
    — An' I've loved thee for it,
Their blood in a woman, to the very last vein.
Tha *must*, though tha tries ter get away.
Tha wants it, and everything else is in vain.
    An' a woman like me loves thee for it.

Maun tha cling to the wa' as tha stan's?
    Ay, an' tha maun.
An' tha looks at me, an' tha understan's.
Yi, tha can go. Tha hates me now.
But tha'lt come again. Because when a man's
Not finished, he hasn't, no matter how.
    Go then, sin' tha maun.

Tha come ter say good-bye ter me.
    Now go then, now then go.
It's ta'en thee seven days ter say it ter me.
Now go an' marry that wench an' see
How long it'll be afore tha'lt be
Weary an' sick o' the likes o' she,
    An' hankerin' for me. But go!

A woman's man tha art, ma lad,
    But it's my sort o' woman.
Go then, thalt' ha'e no peace till ter's had
A go at t'other, for I'm a bad
Sort o' woman for any lad.
    — Ay, it's a rum un!

D. H. LAWRENCE

'Comin thro' the Rye'

Comin thro' the rye, poor body,
Comin thro' the rye,
She draigl't a' her petticoatie
Comin thro' the rye.
Oh Jenny's a' weet, poor body,
Jenny's seldom dry;
She draigl't a' her petticoatie
Comin thro' the rye.

if

Gin a body meet a body,
Comin thro' the rye,
Gin a body kiss a body,
Need a body cry.
Oh Jenny's a' weet, poor body,
Jenny's seldom dry;
She draigl't a' her petticoatie
Comin thro' the rye.

Gin a body meet a body
Comin thro' the glen,
Gin a body kiss a body
Need the warld ken!
Oh Jenny's a' weet, poor body,
Jenny's seldom dry;
She draigl't a' her petticoatie
Comin thro' the rye.

ROBERT BURNS

Will Ye Na Can Ye Na Let Me Be

There liv'd a wife in Whistle Cockpen
will ye na can ye na let me be
ale   she brews gude yill for gentlemen
and ay she waggit it wantonlie

wet   the night blew sair wi wind and weet
will ye na can ye na let me be
to the best room   she shawd the traveller ben to sleep
and ay she waggit it wantonlie

she saw a sight aboon his knee
will ye na can ye na let me be
she wadna wanted it for three
and ay she waggit it wantonlie

o whare live ye and what's your trade
will ye na can ye na let me be
I am a thresher gude he said
and ay she waggit it wantonlie

tools   and that's my flail and workin graith
will ye na can ye na let me be
and noble tools quo she by my faith
and ay she waggit it wantonlie

brew   I wad gie a browst the best I hae
will ye na can ye na let me be
set of tools   for a gude darge o' graith like thae
and ay she waggit it wantonlie

I wad sell the hair frae aff my tail
will ye na can ye na let me be
to buy our Andrew siccan a flail
and ay she waggit it wantonlie

ANON

The Good-Morrow

I wonder by my troth, what thou, and I
Did, till we lov'd, were we not wean'd till then?
But suck'd on countrey pleasures, childishly?
Or snorted we in the seaven sleepers den?
T'was so; But this, all pleasures fancies bee.
If ever any beauty I did see,
Which I desir'd, and got, t'was but a dreame of
    thee.

And now good morrow to our waking soules,
Which watch not one another out of feare;
For love, all love of other sights controules,
And makes one little roome, an every where.
Let sea-discoverers to new worlds have gone,
Let Maps to other, worlds on worlds have
    showne,
Let us possesse one world, each hath one, and is
    one.

My face in thine eye, thine in mine appeares,
And true plaine hearts doe in the faces rest,
Where can we finde two better hemispheares
Without sharpe North, without declining West?
What ever dyes, was not mixt equally;
If our two loves be one, or, thou and I
Love so alike, that none doe slacken, none can die.

JOHN DONNE

'Green sleeves and tartan ties'

Green sleeves and tartan ties
mark my true love whare she lies
I'll be at her or she rise
my fiddle and I tegither

be it by the chrystal burn
be it by the milkwhite thorn
I shall rouse her in the morn
my fiddle and I tegither

ANON

from The Bothie of Tober-Na-Vuolich

I have been kissed before, she added, blushing
  slightly,
I have been kissed more than once by Donald my
  cousin, and others;
It is the way of the lads, and I make up my mind
  not to mind it;
But Mr Philip, last night, and from you, it was
  different quite, Sir.
When I think of all that, I am shocked and
  terrified at it.
Yes, it is dreadful to me.
                She paused, but quickly continued,
Smiling almost fiercely, continued, looking
  upward.
You are too strong, you see, Mr Philip! just like
  the sea there,
Which *will* come, through the straits and all
  between the mountains,
Forcing its great strong tide into every nook and
  inlet,
Getting far in, up the quiet stream of sweet
  inland water,
Sucking it up, and stopping it, turning it, driving
  it backward,
Quite preventing its own quiet running: and
  then, soon after,
Back it goes off, leaving weeds on the shore, and
  wrack and uncleanness:
And the poor burn in the glen tries again its
  peaceful running,
But it is brackish and tainted, and all its banks in
  disorder.
That was what I dreamt all last night. I was the
  burnie,

Trying to get along through the tyrannous brine,
    and could not;
I was confined and squeezed in the coils of the
    great salt tide, that
Would mix-in itself with me, and change me; I
    felt myself changing;
And I struggled, and screamed, I believe, in my
    dream. It was dreadful.
You are too strong, Mr Philip! I am but a poor
    slender burnie,
Used to the glens and the rocks, the rowan and
    birch of the woodies,
Quite unused to the great salt sea; quite afraid
    and unwilling.

ARTHUR HUGH CLOUGH

Moder Phoebe

Old moder Phoebe how happy you be
when you sit under the jinniper tree
oh the jinniper tree so sweet
take this ol hat an keep you head warm
tree an four kisses will do you no harm
it will do a great good te you

ANON

Cushie Butterfield

bargeman

Aa's a broken-hairted keelman, and Aa's ower
   heid in love
Wiv a young lass in Gyetside an' Aa caal hor me
   dove.
Hor nyem's Cushie Butterfield, an' she sells yaller
   clay,
An' hor cousin is a muckman, an' they caal him
   Tom Grey.
     She's a big lass, an' a bonny lass,
       An' she likes hor beor,
      An' they caal hor Cushie Butterfield,
        An' Aa wish she wes heor.

Hor eyes is like two holes in a blanket bornt
   through,
Hor broos in a mornin wad spyen a young coo,
An' when Aa hear hor shoutin: 'Will ye buy ony
   clay?'
Like a candyman's trumpet, it steals me heart
   away.

Ye'll oft see her doon at Sangit when the fresh
   harrin comes in.
She's like a bag o'sawdust, tied roond wiv a
   string.
She wears big galoshes tee, an' hor stockins once
   wes white,
lilac   An' hor bedgoon it's laelock, an' hor hat's nivor
   strite.

When Aa axed hor te marry me she started te
  laugh;
'Noo, nyen o'yer monkey tricks, for Aa like ne
  sich chaff.'
Then she started a-blubbin, an' she roared like a
  bull,
An' the cheps on the Quay says Aa's nowt but a
  fyeul.

She says the chep that gets hor must wark ivory
  day,
An' when he comes hyem at neets he must gan
  an' seek clay,
An' when he's away seekin, she'll myek balls an'
  sing:
O weel may the keel row that ma laddie's in.
    She's a big lass, an' a bonny lass,
        An' she likes hor beor,
      An' they caal hor Cushie Butterfield,
          An' Aa wish she wes heor.

GEORGE RIDLEY

Hold my Rooster

Hold my rooster hold my hen
pray don't touch my Grecian Bend

hold my bonnet hold my shawl
pray don't touch my waterfall

hold my hands by the fingertips
but pray don't touch my sweet little lips

ANON

A Pitman's Lovesong

Aw wish my lover she was a cherry
growing upon yon cherry tree
and aw mysel a bonny blackbird
how aw wad peck that cherry cherree

Aw wish my lover she was a red rose
growing upon yon garden wa'
and aw mysel was a butterflee
O on that red rosie aw wad fa'

Aw wish my lover she was a fish
sooming doon in the saut sea
and aw mysel was a fisher lad
O aw wad catch her reet cunningly

chest   Aw wish my lover was in a kist
and aw mysel to carry the key
then aw wad gan tiv her when aw had list
and bear my hinny good company

Aw wish my love she was a grey ewe
side   grazing by yonder river seid
and aw mysel a bonny black tup
ride   O on that ewie how aw wad reid

O she's bonny she's wondrous canny
O she's well far'd to see
for the mair aw think on her my love's strong
    upon her
and under her apron fain wad aw be

Aw wish my lover she was a bee skep
and aw mysel a bumble bee
that aw might be a lodger within her
she's sweeter than honey or honeycomb tea

Aw wish my lover was a ripe turd
ditchside smoking doon in yon dyke seid
an aw mysel was a shitten flee
dried aw'd sook her all up before she was dreid

O my hinny my bonny hinny
o my hinny my bonny hinnee
the mair aw think on her my heart's set upon her
she's fairer than ever she used to be

ANON

Lines in the Corner of a Manuscript

Thow art pretty but unconstant
too too lovely to be true
thy Affections in an instant
are still struggling to be new
            this and that
                and here and there
always in thy thoughts appear

ANON

The Canonization

For Godsake hold your tongue, and let me love,
   Or chide my palsie, or my gout,
My five gray haires, or ruin'd fortune flout,
   With wealth your state, your minde with Arts
                                        improve
      Take you a course, get you a place,
         Observe his honour, or his grace,
Or the Kings reall, or his stamped face
   Contemplate, what you will, approve,
      So you will let me love.

Alas, alas, who's injur'd by my love?
  What merchants ships have my sighs drown'd?
Who saies my teares have overflow'd his ground?
  When did my colds a forward spring remove?
    When did the heats which my veines fill
    Adde one more, to the plaguie Bill?
Soldiers finde warres, and Lawyers finde out still
  Litigious men, which quarrels move,
  Though she and I do love.

Call us what you will, wee are made such by
                           love;
  Call her one, mee another flye,
We'are Tapers too, and at our owne cost die,
  And wee in us finde the'Eagle and the dove,
    The Phœnix ridle hath more wit
    By us, we two being one, are it.
So, to one neutrall thing both sexes fit.
  Wee dye and rise the same, and prove
  Mysterious by this love.

Wee can dye by it, if not live by love,
  And if unfit for tombes and hearse
Our legends bee, it will be fit for verse;
  And if no peece of Chronicle wee prove,
    We'll build in sonnets pretty roomes;
    As well a well wrought urne becomes
The greatest ashes, as halfe-acre tombes,
  And by these hymnes, all shall approve
  Us *Canoniz'd* for Love.

And thus invoke us; You whom reverend love
   Made one anothers hermitage;
You, to whom love was peace, that now is rage,
   Who did the whole worlds soule contract, &
                            drove
     Into the glasses of your eyes
     So made such mirrors, and such spies,
That they did all to you epitomize,
   Countries, Townes, Courts: Beg from above
   A patterne of our love.

JOHN DONNE

First Sight of Her and After

A day is drawing to its fall
   I had not dreamed to see;
The first of many to enthrall
   My spirit, will it be?
Or is this eve the end of all
   Such new delight for me?

I journey home: the pattern grows
   Of moonshades on the way:
'Soon the first quarter, I suppose,'
   Sky-glancing travellers say;
I realize that it, for those,
   Has been a common day.

THOMAS HARDY

Brown Skin Girl

                    (yes yes
                    yeah)

Mmmmmmmmmmmmmmm
Mmmmmm mmmm mm
Now I got a brown skin girl
With her front tooth crowned with gold
            (take your time and make this one right
            'cause it's the best one you got)
I got a brown skin woman
With her front tooth crowned with gold
She got a lien on my body
And a mortgage on my soul

Now friend don't never let your good girl
Fix you like this woman got me
            (yes yes yes yes)
Friend don't never let your good girl
Fix you like this woman got me
            (how's she got you did)
Got me stone crazy 'bout her
As a doggone fool can be

Now I ain't gonna tell no body,
Baby, 'bout the way you do
            (take your time now and play it right)
Ain't gonna tell no body,
Baby, 'bout the way you do
            (how you got – to – how'd I do)
Say you always keep some
Some fat mouse following you
            (yeah: heh heh heh)

Now I done told you once now baby now
Ain't gonna tell you no more
Mmmm I told you once, baby,
Ain't gonna tell you no more
          (why?)
Next time I have to tell you
I'm sure gonna let you go

Now when you get you one of them funny
                                        women
          (take your time now)
She won't do to trust
Get you a two-by-four
And I swear you can scratch the stuff
Mmmmmmmmmmm
Baby, now that's all I want
Just a little bit of loving,
And then you can be gone

TOMMY McCLENNAN

from Goblin Market

'Good folk,' said Lizzie,
Mindful of Jeanie:
'Give me much and many:' –
Held out her apron,
Tossed them her penny.
'Nay, take a seat with us,
Honour and eat with us,'
They answered grinning:
'Our feast is but beginning.
Night yet is early,
Warm and dew-pearly,
Wakeful and starry:
Such fruits as these
No man can carry;

Half their bloom would fly,
Half their dew would dry,
Half their flavour would pass by.
Sit down and feast with us,
Be welcome guest with us,
Cheer you and rest with us.' –
'Thank you,' said Lizzie: 'But one waits
At home alone for me:
So without further parleying,
If you will not sell me any
Of your fruits tho' much and many,
Give me back my silver penny
I tossed you for a fee.' –
They began to scratch their pates,
No longer wagging, purring,
But visibly demurring,
Grunting and snarling.
One called her proud,
Cross-grained, uncivil;
Their tones waxed loud,
Their looks were evil.
Lashing their tails
They trod and hustled her,
Elbowed and jostled her,
Clawed with their nails,
Barking, mewing, hissing, mocking,
Tore her gown and soiled her stocking,
Twitched her hair out by the roots,
Stamped upon her tender feet,
Held her hands and squeezed their fruits
Against her mouth to make her eat.
White and golden Lizzie stood,
Like a lily in a flood, –
Like a rock of blue-veined stone
Lashed by tides obstreperously, –
Like a beacon left alone
In a hoary roaring sea,
Sending up a golden fire, –

Like a fruit-crowned orange-tree
White with blossoms honey-sweet
Sore beset by wasp and bee, –
Like a royal virgin town
Topped with gilded dome and spire
Close beleaguered by a fleet
Mad to tug her standard down.

One may lead a horse to water,
Twenty cannot make him drink.
Tho' the goblins cuffed and caught her,
Coaxed and fought her,
Bullied and besought her,
Scratched her, pinched her black as ink,
Kicked and knocked her,
Mauled and mocked her,
Lizzie uttered not a word;
Would not open lip from lip
Lest they should cram a mouthful in:
But laughed in heart to feel the drip
Of juice that syrupped all her face,
And lodged in dimples of her chin,
And streaked her neck which quaked like curd.
At last the evil people
Worn out by her resistance
Flung back her penny, kicked their fruit
Along whichever road they took,
Not leaving root or stone or shoot;
Some writhed into the ground,
Some dived into the brook
With ring and ripple,
Some scudded on the gale without a sound,
Some vanished in the distance.
In a smart, ache, tingle,
Lizzie went her way;
Knew not was it night or day;
Sprang up the bank, tore thro' the furze,
Threaded copse and dingle,

And heard her penny jingle
Bouncing in her purse,
Its bounce was music to her ear.
She ran and ran
As if she feared some goblin man
Dogged her with gibe or curse
Or something worse:
But not one goblin skurried after,
Nor was she pricked by fear;
The kind heart made her windy-paced
That urged her home quite out of breath with
    haste
And inward laughter.

She cried 'Laura,' up the garden,
'Did you miss me?
Come and kiss me.
Never mind my bruises,
Hug me, kiss me, suck my juices
Squeezed from goblin fruits for you,
Goblin pulp and goblin dew.
Eat me, drink me, love me;
Laura, make much of me:
For your sake I have braved the glen
And had to do with goblin merchant men.'

Laura started from her chair,
Flung her arms up in the air,
Clutched her hair:
'Lizzie, Lizzie, have you tasted
For my sake the fruit forbidden?
Must your light like mine be hidden,
Your young life like mine be wasted,
Undone in mine undoing
And ruined in my ruin,
Thirsty, cankered, goblin-ridden?' –
She clung about her sister,
Kissed and kissed and kissed her:

Tears once again
Refreshed her shrunken eyes,
Dropping like rain
After long sultry drouth;
Shaking with aguish fear, and pain,
She kissed and kissed her with a hungry mouth.

Her lips began to scorch,
That juice was wormwood to her tongue,
She loathed the feast:
Writhing as one possessed she leaped and sung,
Rent all her robe, and wrung
Her hands in lamentable haste,
And beat her breast.
Her locks streamed like the torch
Borne by a racer at full speed,
Or like the mane of horses in their flight,
Or like an eagle when she stems the light
Straight toward the sun,
Or like a caged thing freed,
Or like a flying flag when armies run.

Swift fire spread thro' her veins, knocked at her
    heart,
Met the fire smouldering there
And overbore its lesser flame;
She gorged on bitterness without a name:
Ah! fool, to choose such part
Of soul-consuming care!
Sense failed in the mortal strife:
Like the watch-tower of a town
Which an earthquake shatters down,
Like a lightning-stricken mast,
Like a wind-uprooted tree
Spun about,
Like a foam-topped waterspout
Cast down headlong in the sea,
She fell at last;

Pleasure past and anguish past,
Is it death or is it life?

Life out of death.
That night long Lizzie watched by her,
Counted her pulse's flagging stir,
Felt for her breath,
Held water to her lips, and cooled her face
With tears and fanning leaves:
But when the first birds chirped about their
    eaves,
And early reapers plodded to the place
Of golden sheaves,
And dew-wet grass
Bowed in the morning winds so brisk to pass,
And new buds with new day
Opened of cup-like lilies on the stream,
Laura awoke as from a dream,
Laughed in the innocent old way,
Hugged Lizzie but not twice or thrice;
Her gleaming locks showed not one thread of
    grey,
Her breath was sweet as May
And light danced in her eyes.

Days, weeks, months, years
Afterwards, when both were wives
With children of their own;
Their mother-hearts beset with fears,
Their lives bound up in tender lives;
Laura would call the little ones
And tell them of her early prime,
Those pleasant days long gone
Of not-returning time:
Would talk about the haunted glen,
The wicked, quaint fruit-merchant men,
Their fruits like honey to the throat
But poison in the blood;

(Men sell not such in any town:)
Would tell them how her sister stood
In deadly peril to do her good,
And win the fiery antidote:
Then joining hands to little hands
Would bid them cling together,
'For there is no friend like a sister
In calm or stormy weather;
To cheer one on the tedious way,
To fetch one if one goes astray,
To lift one if one totters down,
To strengthen whilst one stands.'

CHRISTINA ROSSETTI

'What makes me write'

What makes me write my dearest Freind you
   aske
For our Sex always thought too great a taske
I grant you this yet 'tis no ill spent time
And my thoughts natur'ly fall into Rime
Rude and unpolish't from my pen they flow
So artless I my native tongue scarce know
Learning the Wit & Judgment must improve
Refine the verse and tender passion move
Whilst me no muse assists nor God of Love
Like those whose hearts with suden greife oprest
No kind freind near on whose lov'd constant
   Breast
Leening their drooping Heads they may complain
To Groves which no return can make again
They sigh their Woes to ease theyr killing pain
So whilst in Solitude the days I pass
Paper I make my Freind & minds true Glass
To that my selfe unbosome free from fear
Of a false womans tongue or Lissening eare

Blessing their Fate who your dear Sight enjoye
Pleasures their hours their happy hours imploy
This to us Rurall Nimphs is now deny'd
A life wch is you know my humble share
Free from Ambition nor yet clog'd with care
Nor need I tell you Freind this dismall truth
How vice & folly has possest our youth
So empty is our Sex, yet so vain grow'n
And more debauch't the other ne're were known
Out of such Company whats to be brought
Scandal or nonsense not one solid thought
With joy I from these noysy crouds retire
And from my thoughts of my owne Heart inquire
Shou'd we not to ourselves this great debt pay
The little time that fleeting Life does stay
Wear worthless if unthinking thrown away
Then I my secret thoughts colect & write
Cause this improves me, most does most delight
And whilst with innocence my time I spend
That soonest leads to the proposed end
No guilty blush my cheekes dye to impart
These lines my Freind chast as the Authors Heart
Happy if they can answere your desire
Tho they in flames bright as your eyes expire

HESTER WYAT

from The Spinster's Sweet-Arts

Robby, git down wi'tha, wilt tha? let Steevie
    coom oop o' my knee.
Steevie, my lad, thou 'ed very nigh been the
    Steevie fur me!
Robby wur fust to be sewer, 'e wur burn an' bred
    i' the 'ouse,
But thou be es 'ansom a tabby es iver patted a
    mouse.

An' I beänt not vaäin, but I knaws I 'ed led tha a
    quieter life
Nor her wi' the hepitaph yonder! 'A faäithful an'
    loovin' wife!'
An' 'cos o' thy farm by the beck, an' thy
    windmill oop o' the croft,
Tha thowt tha would marry ma, did tha? but
    that wur a bit ower soft,
Thaw thou was es soäber es daäy, wi' a niced red
    faäce, an' es cleän
Es a shillin' fresh fro' the mint wi' a bran-new
    'eäd o' the Queeän,
An' thy farmin' es cleän es thysen, fur, Steevie,
    tha kep' it sa neät
That I niver not spied sa much es a poppy along
    wi' the wheät,
An' the wool of a thistle a-flyin' an' seeädin' tha
    haäted to see;

earwig

'Twur es bad es a battle-twig 'ere i' my oän blue
    chaumber to me.
Ay, roob thy whiskers ageän ma, fur I could 'a
    taäen to tha well,
But fur thy bairns, poor Steevie, a bouncin' boy
    an' a gell.

An' thou was es fond o' thy bairns es I be mysen
    o' my cats,
But I niver not wished fur childer, I hevn't naw
    likin' fur brats;
Pretty anew when ya dresses 'em oop, an' they
    goäs fur a walk,
Or sits wi' their 'ands afoor 'em, an' doesn't not
    'inder the talk!

shit

But their bottles o' pap, an' their mucky bibs, an'
    the clats an' the clouts,
An' their mashin' their toys to pieäces an'
    maäkin' ma deäf wi' their shouts,

An' hallus a-joompin' about ma as if they was set
 upo' springs,
An' a haxin' ma hawkard questions, an' saäyin'
 ondecent things,
An' a-callin' ma 'hugly' mayhap to my faäce, or a
 teärin' my gown –
Dear! dear! dear! I mun part them Tommies –
 Steevie git down.

Ye be wuss nor the men-tommies, you. I telled
 ya, na moor o' that!
Tom, lig theere o' the cushion, an' tother Tom
 'ere o' the mat.

Theere! I ha' mastered *them*! Hed I married the
 Tommies – O Lord,
To loove an' obaäy the Tommies! I couldn't 'a
 stuck by my word.
To be hordered about, an' waäked, when
 Molly 'd put out the light,
By a man coomin' in wi' a hiccup at ony hour o'
 the night!
An' the taäble staäined wi' 'is aäle, an' the mud
 o' 'is boots o' the stairs,
An' the stink o' 'is pipe i' the 'ouse, an' the mark
 o' is 'eäd o' the chairs!
An' noän o' my four sweet-arts 'ud 'a let me 'a
 hed my oän waäy,
Sa I likes 'em best wi' taäils when they 'evn't a
 word to saäy.

An' I sits i' my oän little parlour, an' sarved by
 my oän little lass,
Wi' my oän little garden outside, an' my oän bed
asparagus o' sparrow-grass,
An' my oän door-poorch wi' the woodbine an'
 jessmine a-dressin' it greeän,
An' my oän fine Jackman i' purple a roäbin' the
 'ouse like a Queeän.

An' the little gells bobs to ma hoffens es I be
    abroad i' the laänes,
When I goäs fur to coomfut the poor es be down
    wi' their haäches an' their paäins:
An' a haäf-pot o' jam or a mossel o' meät when
    it beänt too dear,
They maäkes ma a graäter Laädy nor 'er i' the
    mansion theer,
Hes 'es hallus to hax of a man how much to
    spare or to spend;
An' a spinster I be an' I will be, if soä pleäse
    God, to the hend.

Mew! mew! – Bess wi' the milk! what ha maäde
    our Molly sa laäte?
It should 'a been 'ere by seven, an' theere – it be
    strikin' height –
'Cushie wur craäzed fur 'er cauf' well – I 'eärd
    'er a maäkin' 'er moän,
An' I thowt to mysen 'thank God that I hevn't
    naw cauf o' my oän.'
Theere!
    Set it down!
        Now Robby!
            You Tommies shall waäit tonight
Till Robby an' Steevie 'es 'ed their lap – an' it
    sarves ye right.

ALFRED TENNYSON

A Toccata of Galuppi's

I

Oh Galuppi, Baldassaro, this is very sad to find!
I can hardly misconceive you; it would prove me
    deaf and blind;
But although I take your meaning, 'tis with such
    a heavy mind!

II

Here you come with your old music, and here's
    all the good it brings.
What, they lived once thus at Venice where the
    merchants were the kings,
Where Saint Mark's is, where the Doges used to
    wed the sea with rings?

III

Ay, because the sea's the street there; and 't is
    arched by . . . what you call
. . . Shylock's bridge with houses on it, where
    they kept the carnival:
I was never out of England — it's as if I saw it all.

IV

Did young people take their pleasure when the
    sea was warm in May?
Balls and masks begun at midnight, burning ever
    to mid-day,
When they made up fresh adventures for the
    morrow, do you say?

V

Was a lady such a lady, cheeks so round and lips
   so red, –
On her neck the small face buoyant, like a bell-
   flower on its bed,
O'er the breast's superb abundance where a man
   might base his head?'

VI

Well, and it was graceful of them – they'd break
   talk off and afford
– She, to bite her mask's black velvet – he, to
   finger on his sword,
While you sat and played Toccatas, stately at the
   clavichord?

VII

What? Those lesser thirds so plaintive, sixths
   diminished, sigh on sigh,
Told them something? Those suspensions, those
   solutions – 'Must we die?'
Those commiserating sevenths – 'Life might last!
   we can but try!'

VIII

'Were you happy?' – 'Yes.' – 'And are you still as
   happy?' – 'Yes. And you?'
– 'Then, more kisses!' – 'Did *I* stop them, when a
   million seemed so few?'
Hark, the dominant's persistence till it must be
   answered to!

IX

So, an octave struck the answer. Oh, they praised
    you, I dare say!
'Brave Galuppi! that was music! good alike at
    grave and gay!
'I can always leave off talking when I hear a
    master play!'

X

Then they left you for their pleasure: till in due
    time, one by one,
Some with lives that came to nothing, some with
    deeds as well undone,
Death stepped tacitly and took them where they
    never see the sun.

XI

But when I sit down to reason, think to take my
    stand nor swerve,
While I triumph o'er a secret wrung from
    nature's close reserve,
In you come with your cold music till I creep
    thro' every nerve.

XII

Yes, you, like a ghostly cricket, creaking where a
    house was burned:
'Dust and ashes, dead and done with, Venice
    spent what Venice earned.
'The soul, doubtless, is immortal – where a soul
    can be discerned.

XIII

'Yours for instance: you know physics,
  something of geology,
'Mathematics are your pastime; souls shall rise in
  their degree;
'Butterflies may dread extinction, – you'll not die,
  it cannot be!

XIV

'As for Venice and her people, merely born to
  bloom and drop,
'Here on earth they bore their fruitage, mirth and
  folly were the crop:
'What of soul was left, I wonder, when the
  kissing had to stop?

XV

'Dust and ashes!' So you creak it, and I want the
  heart to scold.
Dear dead women, with such hair, too – what's
  become of all the gold
Used to hang and brush their bosoms? I feel
  chilly and grown old.

ROBERT BROWNING

from The Bride-Night Fire

'O Tim, my *own* Tim I must call 'ee – I will!
  All the world has turned round on me so!
Can you help her who loved 'ee, though acting so
                                                    ill?
Can you pity her misery – feel for her still?
When worse than her body so quivering and chill
  Is her heart in its winter o' woe!

might

    'I think I mid almost ha' borne it,' she said,
      'Had my griefs one by one come to hand;

that rascal

But O, to be slave to thik husbird, for bread,
And then, upon top o' that, driven to wed,
And then, upon top o' that, burnt out o' bed,
    Is more than my nater can stand!'

Like a lion 'ithin en Tim's spirit outsprung –
(Tim had a great soul when his feelings were
                  wrung) –
    'Feel for 'ee, dear Barbree?' he cried;
And his warm working-jacket then straightway
                  he flung

carried

Round about her, and horsed her by jerks, till
                  she clung
Like a chiel on a gipsy, her figure uphung
    By the sleeves that he tightly had tied.

dung-heaps
stumbled
bridle-path

Over piggeries, and mixens, and apples, and hay,
    They lumpered straight into the night;
And finding ere long where a halter-path lay,
Sighted Tim's house by dawn, on'y seen on their
                  way
By a naibour or two who were up wi' the day,
    But who gathered no clue to the sight.

Then tender Tim Tankens he searched here and
                  there
    For some garment to clothe her fair skin;
But though he had breeches and waistcoats to
                  spare,
He had nothing quite seemly for Barbree to wear,

numbed

Who, half shrammed to death, stood and cried
                  on a chair

quandary

    At the caddle she found herself in.

There was one thing to do, and that one thing he
                                                did,
   He lent her some clothes of his own,
And she took 'em perforce; and while swiftly she
                                               slid
Them upon her Tim turned to the winder, as bid,
Thinking, 'O that the picter my duty keeps hid
   To the sight o' my eyes mid be shown!'

loft/hidden   In the tallet he stowed her; there huddied she lay,
                          Shortening sleeves, legs, and tails to her limbs;
                       But most o' the time in a mortal bad way,
                       Well knowing that there'd be the divel to pay
                       If 'twere found that, instead o' the element's
                                                               prey,
                          She was living in lodgings at Tim's.

'Where's the tranter?' said men and boys; 'where
                                          can he be?'
   'Where's the tranter?' said Barbree alone.
'Where on e'th is the tranter?' said everybod-y:
They sifted the dust of his perished roof-tree,
   And all they could find was a bone.

Then the uncle cried, 'Lord, pray have mercy on
                                               me!'
   And in terror began to repent.
But before 'twas complete, and till sure she was
                                               free,
Barbree drew up her loft-ladder, tight turned her
                                               key –
Tim bringing up breakfast and dinner and tea –
   Till the news of her hiding got vent.

Then followed the custom-kept rout, shout, and
            flare

satirical procession　　Of a skimmity-ride through the naibourhood, ere
old　　 Folk had proof o' wold Sweatley's decay.
Whereupon decent people all stood in a stare,
Saying Tim and his lodger should risk it, and
              pair:
So he took her to church. An' some laughing lads
              there
Cried to Tim, 'After Sweatley!' She said, 'I
           declare
    I stand as a maiden to-day!'

THOMAS HARDY

Weddings

A weddin' a woo a clog an' a shoe
a pot full o'porridge an' away they goo

ANON

from Christabel

'Tis the middle of night by the castle clock,
And the owls have awakened the crowing cock;
Tu – whit! – Tu – whoo!
And hark, again! the crowing cock,
How drowsily it crew.
Sir Leoline, the Baron rich,

Hath a toothless mastiff bitch;
From her kennel beneath the rock
She maketh answer to the clock,
Four for the quarters, and twelve for the hour;
Ever and aye, by shine and shower,
Sixteen short howls, not over loud;
Some say, she sees my lady's shroud.

Is the night chilly and dark?
The night is chilly, but not dark.
The thin gray cloud is spread on high,
It covers but not hides the sky.
The moon is behind, and at the full;
And yet she looks both small and dull.
The night is chill, the cloud is gray:
'Tis a month before the month of May,
And the Spring comes slowly up this way.

The lovely lady, Christabel,
Whom her father loves so well,
What makes her in the wood so late,
A furlong from the castle gate?
She had dreams all yesternight
Of her own betrothéd knight;
And she in the midnight wood will pray
For the weal of her lover that's far away.

She stole along, she nothing spoke,
The sighs she heaved were soft and low,
And naught was green upon the oak
But moss and rarest misletoe:
She kneels beneath the huge oak tree,
And in silence prayeth she.

The lady sprang up suddenly.
The lovely lady, Christabel!
It moaned as near, as near can be,
But what it is she cannot tell. –
On the other side it seems to be,
Of the huge, broad-breasted, old oak tree.

SAMUEL TAYLOR COLERIDGE

'I have no Life but this'

I have no Life but this –
To lead it here –
Nor any Death – but lest
Dispelled from there –

Nor tie to Earths to come –
Nor Action new –
Except through this extent –
The Realm of you –

EMILY DICKINSON

from Songs for a Colored Singer

A washing hangs upon the line,
    but it's not mine.
None of the things that I can see
    belong to me.
The neighbors got a radio with an aerial;
    we got a little portable.
They got a lot of closet space;
    we got a suitcase.

I say, 'Le Roy, just how much are we owing?
Something I can't comprehend,
the more we got the more we spend . . .'
He only answers, 'Let's get going.'
Le Roy, you're earning too much money now.

I sit and look at our backyard
    and find it very hard.
What have we got for all his dollars and cents?
    – A pile of bottles by the fence.
He's faithful and he's kind
    but he sure has an inquiring mind.
He's seen a lot; he's bound to see the rest,
    and if I protest

Le Roy answers with a frown,
    'Darling, when I earns I spends.
The world is wide; it still extends . . .
I'm going to get a job in the next town.'
Le Roy, you're earning too much money now.

ELIZABETH BISHOP

Somewhere or Other

Somewhere or other there must surely be
    The face not seen, the voice not heard,
The heart that not yet – never yet – ah me!
    Made answer to my word.

Somewhere or other, may be near or far;
    Past land and sea, clean out of sight;
Beyond the wandering moon, beyond the star
    That tracks her night by night.

Somewhere or other, may be far or near;
  With just a wall, a hedge, between;
With just the last leaves of the dying year
  Fallen on a turf grown green.

CHRISTINA ROSSETTI

from Amours de Voyage, I

Claude to Eustace

Dear Eustatio, I write that you may write me an
  answer,
Or at the least to put us again *en rapport* with
  each other.
Rome disappoints me much, — St Peter's,
  perhaps, in especial;
Only the Arch of Titus and view from the
  Lateran please me:
This, however, perhaps, is the weather, which
  truly is horrid.
Greece must be better, surely; and yet I am
  feeling so spiteful,
That I could travel to Athens, to Delphi, and
  Troy, and Mount Sinai,
Though but to see with my eyes that these are
  vanity also.
    Rome disappoints me much; I hardly as yet
        understand, but
Rubbishy seems the word that most exactly
  would suit it.
All the foolish destructions, and all the sillier
  savings,
All the incongruous things of past incompatible
  ages,
Seem to be treasured up here to make fools of
  present and future.

Would to Heaven the old Goths had made a
    cleaner sweep of it!
Would to Heaven some new ones would come
    and destroy these churches!
However, one can live in Rome as also in
    London.
Rome is better than London, because it is other
    than London.
It is a blessing, no doubt, to be rid, at least for a
    time, of
All one's friends and relations, – yourself (forgive
    me!) included, –
All the *assujettissement* of having been what one
    has been,
What one thinks one is, or thinks that others
    suppose one;
Yet, in despite of all, we turn like fools to the
    English.
Vernon has been my fate; who is here the same
    that you knew him, –
Making the tour, it seems, with friends of the
    name of Trevellyn.

Claude to Eustace

These are the facts. The uncle, the elder brother,
    the squire (a
Little embarrassed, I fancy), resides in a family
    place in
Cornwall, of course; 'Papa is in business,' Mary
    informs me;
He's a good sensible man, whatever his trade is.
    The mother
Is – shall I call it fine? – herself she would tell
    you refined, and
Greatly, I fear me, looks down on my bookish
    and maladroit manners;

Somewhat affecteth the blue; would talk to me
  often of poets;
Quotes, which I hate, Childe Harold; but also
  appreciates Wordsworth;
Sometimes adventures on Schiller; and then to
  religion diverges;
Questions me much about Oxford; and yet, in
  her loftiest flights, still
Grates the fastidious ear with the slightly
  mercantile accent.

  Is it contemptible, Eustace, – I'm perfectly
    ready to think so, –
Is it, – the horrible pleasure of pleasing inferior
  people?
I am ashamed my own self; and yet true it is, if
  disgraceful,
That for the first time in life I am living and
  moving with freedom.
I, who never could talk to the people I meet with
  my uncle, –
I, who have always failed, – I, trust me, can suit
  the Trevellyns;
I, believe me, – great conquest, – am liked by the
  country bankers.
And I am glad to be liked, and like in return very
  kindly.
So it proceeds; *Laissez faire, laissez aller*, – such
  is the watchword.
Well, I know there are thousands as pretty and
  hundreds as pleasant,
Girls by the dozen as good, and girls in
  abundance with polish
Higher and manners more perfect than Susan or
  Mary Trevellyn.
Well, I know, after all, it is only juxtaposition, –
Juxtaposition, in short; and what is
  juxtaposition?

Georgina Trevellyn to Louisa

Dearest Louisa, – Inquire, if you please, about
   Mr Claude —.
He has been once at R., and remembers meeting
   the H.s.
Harriet L., perhaps, may be able to tell you
   about him.
It is an awkward youth, but still with very good
   manners;
Not without prospects, we hear; and, George
   says, highly connected.
Georgy declares it absurd, but Mamma is
   alarmed, and insists he has
Taken up strange opinions and may be turning a
   Papist.
Certainly once he spoke of a daily service he
   went to.
'Where?' we asked, and he laughed and
   answered, 'At the Pantheon.'
This was a temple, you know, and now is a
   Catholic church; and
Though it is said that Mazzini has sold it for
   Protestant service,
Yet I suppose the change can hardly as yet be
   effected.
Adieu again, – evermore, my dearest, your loving
   Georgina.

P.S. by Mary Trevellyn

I am to tell you, you say, what I think of our last
   new acquaintance.
Well, then, I think that George has a very fair
   right to be jealous.
I do not like him much, though I do not dislike
   being with him.

He is what people call, I suppose, a superior
    man, and
Certainly seems so to me; but I think he is
    frightfully selfish.

ARTHUR HUGH CLOUGH

from Amours de Voyage, II

Claude to Eustace

I am in love, meantime, you think; no doubt you
    would think so.
I am in love, you say; with those letters, of
    course, you would say so.
I am in love, you declare. I think not so; yet I
    grant you
It is a pleasure, indeed, to converse with this girl.
    Oh, rare gift,
Rare felicity, this! she can talk in a rational way,
    can
Speak upon subjects that really are matters of
    mind and of thinking,
Yet in perfection retain her simplicity; never, one
    moment,
Never, however you urge it, however you tempt
    her, consents to
Step from ideas and fancies and loving sensations
    to those vain
Conscious understandings that vex the minds of
    man-kind.
No, though she talk, it is music; her fingers
    desert not the keys; 'tis
Song, though you hear in the song the articulate
    vocables sounded,

Syllabled singly and sweetly the words of
   melodious meaning.
     I am in love, you say; I do not think so
      exactly.

ARTHUR HUGH CLOUGH

from Amours de Voyage, III

Mary Trevellyn to Miss Roper

Dear Miss Roper, – It seems, George Vernon,
   before we left Rome, said
Something to Mr Claude about what they call his
   attentions.
Susan, two nights ago, for the first time, heard
   this from Georgina.
It is *so* disagreeable and *so* annoying to think of!
If it could only be known, though we may never
   meet him again, that
It was all George's doing, and we were entirely
   unconscious,
It would extremely relieve – Your ever
   affectionate Mary.

P.S. (1)

   Here is your letter arrived this moment, just as
     I wanted.
So you have seen him, – indeed, – and guessed, –
   how dreadfully clever!
What did he really say? and what was your
   answer exactly?
Charming! – but wait for a moment, I haven't
   read through the letter.

P.S. (2)

> Ah, my dearest Miss Roper, do just as you
>   fancy about it.
> If you think it sincerer to tell him I know of it,
>   do so.
> Though I should most extremely dislike it, I
>   know I could manage.
> It is the simplest thing, but surely wholly uncalled
>   for.
> Do as you please; you know I trust implicitly to
>   you.
> Say whatever is right and needful for ending the
>   matter.
> Only don't tell Mr Claude, what I will tell you as
>   a secret,
> That I should like very well to show him myself I
>   forget it.

P.S. (3)

> I am to say that the wedding is finally settled
>   for Tuesday.
> Ah, my dear Miss Roper, you surely, surely can
>   manage
> Not to let it appear that I know of that odious
>   matter.
> It would be pleasanter far for myself to treat it
>   exactly
> As if it had not occurred; and I do not think he
>   would like it.
> I must remember to add, that as soon as the
>   wedding is over
> We shall be off, I believe, in a hurry, and travel
>   to Milan,

There to meet friends of Papa's, I am told, at the
    Croce di Malta;
Then I cannot say whither, but not at present to
    England.

ARTHUR HUGH CLOUGH

from Amours de Voyage, IV

Claude to Eustace, – from Bellaggio

I have but one chance left, – and that is going to
    Florence.
But it is cruel to turn. The mountains seem to
    demand me, –
Peak and valley from far to beckon and motion
    me onward.
Somewhere amid their folds she passes whom
    fain I would follow;
Somewhere among those heights she haply calls
    me to seek her.
Ah, could I hear her call! could I catch the
    glimpse of her raiment!
Turn, however, I must, though it seem I turn to
    desert her;
For the sense of the thing is simply to hurry to
    Florence,
Where the certainty yet may be learnt, I suppose,
    from the Ropers.

ARTHUR HUGH CLOUGH

'Foweles in the frith'

birds/forest

river

go mad

because of the best creature living

Foweles in the frith
the fisses in the flod
and I mon waxe wod
much sorw I walke with
for beste of bon and blod

ANON

'Fforget not yet'

Fforget not yet the tryde entent
of suche a truthe as I haue ment
my gret travayle so gladly spent
                fforget not yet

fforget not yet when fyrst began
the wery lyffe ye know syns whan
the sute the seruys none tell can
                fforgett not yet

fforget not yet the gret assays
the cruell wrong the skornfull ways
the paynfull pacyence in denays
                fforgett not yet

fforget not yet forget not thys
how long ago hathe bene and ys
the mynd that neuer ment amys
                fforget not yet

fforget not then thyn owne aprovyd
the whyche so long hathe the so lovyd
whose stedfast faythe yet neuer movyd
fforget not thys

THOMAS WYATT

'O I hae tint my rosy cheek'

lost

O I hae tint my rosy cheek
likewise my waste sae sma'
woe/skulking

O wae gae by the sodger lown
the sodger did it a'

fuck

O wha'll mow me now my jo
an wha'll mow me now
a sodger wi his bandileers
has banged my belly fu

endure

now I maun thole the scornfu sneer
hussy

o'mony a saucy quine
when curse upon her godly face
her cunt's as merry's mine

our dame hauds up her wanton tail
when it's her lying-in time

as due as she gaes lie
an yet misca's a young thing
the trade if she but try

our dame can lae her ain gudeman
an mow for glutton greed
an yet misca' a poor thing
that's mown for its bread

alake sae sweet a tree as love
sic bitter fruit should bear
alake that e'er a merry arse
salty   should draw a sa'tty tear

but deevil damn the lousy loon
denies the bairn he got
or lea's the merry arse he lo'ed
to wear a ragged coat!

ANON

'Thenmy of liff decayer of all kynde'

Thenmy of liff decayer of all kynde
that with his cold wythers away the grene
this othre nyght me in my bed did fynde
and offered me to rid my fiever clene
and I did graunt so did dispayre me blynde
he drewe his bowe with arrowe sharp and kene
and strake the place where love had hit before
and drave the first dart deper more and more

THOMAS WYATT

Hard Road Blues

Keep on walkin and walkin   talkin to mysel
yes keep on walkin and walkin   talkin to mysel
gal I loves wid somebody else

I got the hard road blues   walkin on down the
    line
oh yes got the hard road blues   walkin on down
    the line
maybe someday my gal will change her mind

its a hard hard road when your baby done
    throwed you down
a hard hard road when your baby done throwed
    you down
gonna keep on walkin from town to town

I'm gonna find my baby   don't think she can't
    be found
gonna find my baby   don't think she can't be
    found
gonna walk this hard road till my mustache
    touch the ground

ANON

The Pine Planters

(Marty South's Reverie)

I

We work here together
    In blast and breeze;
He fills the earth in,
    I hold the trees.

He does not notice
    That what I do
Keeps me from moving
    And chills me through.

He has seen one fairer
I feel by his eye,
Which skims me as though
I were not by.

And since she passed here
He scarce has known
But that the woodland
Holds him alone.

I have worked here with him
Since morning shine,
He busy with his thoughts
And I with mine.

I have helped him so many,
So many days,
But never win any
Small word of praise!

Shall I not sigh to him
That I work on
Glad to be nigh to him
Though hope is gone?

Nay, though he never
Knew love like mine,
I'll bear it ever
And make no sign!

II

From the bundle at hand here
I take each tree,
And set it to stand, here
Always to be;

When, in a second,
    As if from fear
Of life unreckoned
    Beginning here,
It starts a sighing
    Through day and night,
Though while there lying
    'Twas voiceless quite.

It will sigh in the morning,
    Will sigh at noon,
At the winter's warning,
    In wafts of June;
Grieving that never
    Kind Fate decreed
It should for ever
    Remain a seed,
And shun the welter
    Of things without,
Unneeding shelter
    From storm and drought.

Thus, all unknowing
    For whom or what
We set it growing
    In this bleak spot,
It still will grieve here
    Throughout its time,
Unable to leave here,
    Or change its clime;
Or tell the story
    Of us to-day
When, halt and hoary,
    We pass away.

THOMAS HARDY

'O wert thou in the cauld blast'

O wert thou in the cauld blast,
  On yonder lea, on yonder lea;
plaid/quarter   My plaidie to the angry airt,
  I'd shelter thee, I'd shelter thee:
Or did misfortune's bitter storms
  Around thee blaw, around thee blaw,
shelter   Thy bield should be my bosom,
  To share it a', to share it a'.

Or were I in the wildest waste,
  Sae black and bare, sae black and bare,
The desart were a paradise,
  If thou wert there, if thou wert there.
Or were I monarch o' the globe,
  Wi' thee to reign, wi' thee to reign;
The brightest jewel in my crown,
  Wad be my queen, wad be my queen

ROBERT BURNS

The Rantin Dog the Daddie o't

O Wha my babie-clouts will buy,
O Wha will tent me when I cry;
Wha will kiss me where I lie,
The rantin dog the daddie o't.

O Wha will own he did the faut,
O Wha will buy the groanin maut,
O Wha will tell me how to ca't,
The rantin dog the daddie o't.

stool of repentance

When I mount the Creepie-chair,
Wha will sit beside me there,
Gie me Rob, I'll seek nae mair,
The rantin dog the Daddie o't.

talk / on my own
excited / eager

Wha will crack to me my lane;
Wha will mak me fidgin fain;
Wha will kiss me o'er again
The rantin dog the Daddie o't.

ROBERT BURNS

Tess's Lament

I

I would that folk forgot me quite,
   Forgot me quite!
I would that I could shrink from sight,
  And no more see the sun.
Would it were time to say farewell,
To claim my nook, to need my knell,
Time for them all to stand and tell
  Of my day's work as done.

II

Ah! dairy where I lived so long,
   I lived so long;
Where I would rise up staunch and strong,
  And lie down hopefully.
'Twas there within the chimney-seat
He watched me to the clock's slow beat —
Loved me, and learnt to call me Sweet,
  And whispered words to me.

III

And now he's gone; and now he's gone; . . .
                    And now he's gone!
The flowers we potted perhaps are thrown
        To rot upon the farm.
And where we had our supper-fire
May now grow nettle, dock, and briar,
And all the place be mould and mire
        So cozy once and warm.

IV

And it was I who did it all,
                    Who did it all;
'Twas I who made the blow to fall
        On him who thought no guile.
Well, it is finished — past, and he
Has left me to my misery,
And I must take my Cross on me
        For wronging him awhile.

V

How gay we looked that day we wed,
                    That day we wed!
'May joy be with ye!' they all said
door-post   A-standing by the durn.
I wonder what they say o'us now,
And if they know my lot; and how
She feels who milks my favourite cow,
        And takes my place at churn!

VI

It wears me out to think of it,
                    To think of it;
I cannot bear my fate as writ,
        I'd have my life unbe;
Would turn my memory to a blot,
Make every relic of me rot,
My doings be as they were not,
        And gone all trace of me!

THOMAS HARDY

Tired As I Can Be

I worked all the winter
        and I worked all fall
I got to wait till spring
        to get my ashes hauled
                and now I'm tired
                        tired as I can be
                and I'm going back home
                        where these blues don't worry me

I'm a free-hearted woman
        I let you spend my dough
and you never did win
        you kept on asking for more
                and now I'm tired
                        I ain't gonna do it no more
                and when I leave you this time
                        you won't know where I go

My house rent's due
    they done put me out doors
and here you riding 'round here
    in a V-8 Ford
        I done got tired
            of your low-down dirty ways
        and your sister say you been dirty
            dirty all a your days

I never will forget
    when the times was good
I caught you standing out yonder
    in the piney wood
        and now I'm tired
            tired as I can be
        and I'm going back south
        to my used to be

BESSIE JACKSON (LUCILLE BOGAN)

The Collier's Wife

Somebody's knockin' at th' door
    Mother, come down an' see!
— I's think it's nobbut a beggar;
    Say I'm busy.

It's not a beggar, mother; hark
    How 'ard 'e knocks!
spoilt   — Eh, tha'rt a mard-arsed kid,
blows   'E'll gie thee socks!

Shout an' ax what 'e wants,
    I canna come down.
— 'E says, is it Arthur Holliday's?
    — Say Yes, tha clown.

'E says: Tell your mother as 'er mester's
 Got hurt i' th' pit –
What? Oh my Sirs, 'e never says that.
 That's not it!

Come out o' th' way an' let me see!
 Eh, there's no peace!
An' stop thy scraightin', childt,
 Do shut thy face!

'Your mester's 'ad a accident
 An' they ta'ein' 'im i' th' ambulance
Ter Nottingham.' – Eh dear o' me,
 If 'e's not a man for mischance!

Wheer's 'e hurt this time, lad?
 – I dunna know,
They on'y towd me it wor bad –
 It would be so!

Out o' my way, childt! dear o' me, wheer
 'Ave I put 'is clean stockin's an' shirt?
Goodness knows if they'll be able
 To take off 'is pit-dirt!

An' what a moan e'll make! there niver
 Was such a man for fuss
If anything ailed 'im; at any rate
 I shan't 'ave 'im to nuss.

I do 'ope as it's not very bad!
 Eh, what a shame it seems
As some should ha'e hardly a smite o' trouble
 An' others 'as reams!

It's a shame as 'e should be knocked about
 Like this, I'm sure it is!
'E's 'ad twenty accidents, if 'e's 'ad one;
 Owt bad, an' it's his!

There's one thing, we s'll 'ave a peaceful 'ouse f'r
                                        a bit,
        Thank heaven for a peaceful house!
An' there's compensation, sin' it's accident.
        An' club-money – I won't growse.

An' a fork an' a spoon 'e'll want – an' what else?
        I s'll never catch that train!
What a traipse it is, if a man gets hurt!
        I sh'd think 'e'll get right again.

D. H. LAWRENCE

The Shoemakker

My mother sent us to the school
to learn to be a stocking knitter
but Aa was young and played the fool
and married wi a shoemakker
shoemakker   leather cracker
wi all his stinking dirty watter
Aa wish a thousand deaths Aad died
ere Aad wed a shoemakker

donkey's hocks

shiny

his hands are like a cuddy's houghs
his face is like the highlowed leather
his ears are like Aa don't know what
his hair is like a buncha heather
shoemakker   leather cracker

resin, pitch and tallow mixture

stinking kit and rotten leather
Aa wish a thousand deaths Aad died
ere Aad wed a shoemakker

he sent me for a pint of wine
and Aa brought him a pint of watter
but he played me as good a trick
he made my shoes arotten leather
shoemakker   leatherstrapper
three rows arotten leather
balls of wax and stinking watter
who would have a shoemakker?

ANON

'I caught a little ladybird'

I caught a little ladybird
   That flies far away;
I caught a little lady wife
   That is both staid and gay.

Come back, my scarlet ladybird,
   Back from far away;
I weary of my dolly wife,
   My wife that cannot play.

She's such a senseless wooden thing
   She stares the livelong day;
Her wig of gold is stiff and cold
   And cannot change to grey.

CHRISTINA ROSSETTI

from *The Winter's Tale*, Act I, scene 2

To your owne bents dispose you: you'le be
    found,
Be you beneath the Sky: (*Aside*) I am angling
    now,
(Though you perceive me not how I give Lyne)
Goe too, goe too.
How she holds up the Neb? the Byll to him?
And armes her with the boldness of a Wife
To her allowing Husband.
                    Exeunt Polixenes and Hermione
                    Gone already,
Ynch-thick, knee-deepe; ore head and eares a
    fork'd one.
Goe play (Boy) play: thy Mother playes, and I
Play too; but so disgrac'd a part, whose issue
Will hisse me to my Grave: Contempt and
    Clamor
Will be my Knell. Goe play (Boy) play, there
    have been
(Or I am much deceiv'd) Cuckolds ere now,
And many a man there is (even at this present,
Now, while I speake this) holds his Wife by
    th'Arme,
That little thinkes she ha's been sluyc'd in's
    absence,
And his Pond fish'd by his next Neighbor (by
Sir Smile, his Neighbor:) nay, there's comfort
    in't,
Whiles other men have Gates, and those Gates
    open'd
(As mine) against their will. Should all despaire
That have revolted Wives, the tenth of Mankind
Would hang themselves. Physick for't, there's
    none:

It is a bawdy Planet, that will strike
Where 'tis predominant; and 'tis powrefull:
    thinke it:
From East, West, North, and South, be it
    concluded,
No Barricado for a Belly. Know't,
It will let in and out the Enemy,
With bag and baggage: how many thousand on's
Have the Disease, and feele't not. How now Boy?

WILLIAM SHAKESPEARE

'The Iniquity of the Fathers upon the Children'

Oh the rose of keenest thorn!
One hidden summer morn
Under the rose I was born.

I do not guess his name
Who wrought my Mother's shame,
And gave me life forlorn,
But my Mother, Mother, Mother,
I know her from all other.
My Mother pale and mild,
Fair as ever was seen,
She was but scarce sixteen,
Little more than a child,
When I was born
To work her scorn.
With secret bitter throes,
In a passion of secret woes,
She bore me under the rose.

One who my Mother nursed
Took me from the first: —
'O nurse, let me look upon
This babe that costs so dear;
Tomorrow she will be gone:
Other mothers may keep
Their babes awake and asleep,
But I must not keep her here.' —
Whether I know or guess,
I know this not the less.

So I was sent away
That none might spy the truth:
And my childhood waxed to youth
And I left off childish play.
I never cared to play
With the village boys and girls;
And I think they thought me proud,
I found so little to say
And kept so from the crowd:
But I had the longest curls
And I had the largest eyes,
And my teeth were small like pearls;
The girls might flout and scout me,
But the boys would hang about me
In sheepish mooning wise.

Our one-street village stood
A long mile from the town,
A mile of windy down
And bleak one-sided wood,
With not a single house.

Our town itself was small,
With just the common shops,
And throve in its small way.
Our neighbouring gentry reared
The good old-fashioned crops,
And made old-fashioned boasts
Of what John Bull would do
If Frenchman Frog appeared,
And drank old-fashioned toasts,
And made old-fashioned bows
To my Lady at the Hall.

My Lady at the Hall
Is grander than they all:
Hers is the oldest name
In all the neighbourhood;
But the race must die with her
Tho' she's a lofty dame,
For she's unmarried still.
Poor people say she's good
And has an open hand
As any in the land,
And she's the comforter
Of many sick and sad;
My nurse once said to me
That everything she had
Came of my Lady's bounty:
'Tho' she's greatest in the county
She's humble to the poor,
No beggar seeks her door
But finds help presently.
I pray both night and day
For her, and you must pray:
But she'll never feel distress
If needy folk can bless.'

I was a little maid
When here we came to live
From somewhere by the sea.
Men spoke a foreign tongue
There where we used to be
When I was merry and young,
Too young to feel afraid;
The fisher-folk would give
A kind strange word to me,
There by the foreign sea:
I don't know where it was,
But I remember still
Our cottage on a hill,
And fields of flowering grass
On that fair foreign shore.

I liked my old home best,
But this was pleasant too:
So here we made our nest
And here I grew.
And now and then my Lady
In riding past our door
Would nod to Nurse and speak,
Or stoop and pat my cheek;
And I was always ready
To hold the field-gate wide
For my Lady to go thro';
My Lady in her veil
So seldom put aside,
My Lady grave and pale.
I often sat to wonder
Who might my parents be,
For I knew of something under
My simple-seeming state.
Nurse never talked to me
Of mother or of father,
But watched me early and late

With kind suspicious cares:
Or not suspicious, rather
Anxious, as if she knew
Some secret I might gather
And smart for unawares.
Thus I grew.

But Nurse waxed old and grey,
Bent and weak with years.
There came a certain day
That she lay upon her bed
Shaking her palsied head,
With words she gasped to say
Which had to stay unsaid.
Then with a jerking hand
Held out so piteously
She gave a ring to me
Of gold wrought curiously.
A ring which she had worn
Since the day that I was born,
She once had said to me:
I slipped it on my finger;
Her eyes were keen to linger
On my hand that slipped it on;
Then she sighed one rattling sigh
And stared on with sightless eyes: —
The one who loved me was gone.

How long I stayed alone
With the corpse, I never knew,
For I fainted dead as stone:
When I came to life once more
I was down upon the floor,
With neighbours making ado
To bring me back to life.
I heard the sexton's wife
Say: 'Up, my lad, and run
To tell it at the Hall;

She was my Lady's nurse,
And done can't be undone.
I'll watch by this poor lamb.
I guess my Lady's purse
Is always open to such:
I'd run up on my crutch
A cripple as I am,'
(For cramps had vexed her much)
'Rather than this dear heart
Lack one to take her part.'

For days day after day
On my weary bed I lay
Wishing the time would pass;
Oh, so wishing that I was
Likely to pass away:
For the one friend whom I knew
Was dead, I knew no other,
Neither father nor mother;
And I, what should I do?

One day the sexton's wife
Said: 'Rouse yourself, my dear:
My Lady has driven down
From the Hall into the town,
And we think she's coming here.
Cheer up, for life is life.'

But I would not look or speak,
Would not cheer up at all.
My tears were like to fall,
So I turned round to the wall
And hid my hollow cheek
Making as if I slept,
As silent as a stone,
And no one knew I wept.
What was my Lady to me,
The grand lady from the Hall?

She might come, or stay away,
I was sick at heart that day:
The whole world seemed to be
Nothing, just nothing to me,
For aught that I could see.

Yet I listened where I lay:
A bustle came below,
A clear voice said: 'I know;
I will see her first alone,
It may be less of a shock
If she's so weak today:' –
A light hand turned the lock,
A light step crossed the floor,
One sat beside my bed:
But never a word she said.

For me, my shyness grew
Each moment more and more:
So I said never a word
And neither looked nor stirred;
I think she must have heard
My heart go pit-a-pat:
Thus I lay, my Lady sat,
More than a mortal hour –
(I counted one and two
By the house-clock while I lay):
I seemed to have no power
To think of a thing to say,
Or do what I ought to do,
Or rouse myself to a choice.
At last she said: 'Margaret,
Won't you even look at me?'
A something in her voice
Forced my tears to fall at last,
Forced sobs from me thick and fast;
Something not of the past,
Yet stirring memory;

A something new, and yet
Not new, too sweet to last,
Which I never can forget.

I turned and stared at her:
Her cheek showed hollow-pale;
Her hair like mine was fair,
A wonderful fall of hair
That screened her like a veil;
But her height was statelier,
Her eyes had depth more deep;
I think they must have had
Always a something sad,
Unless they were asleep.

While I stared, my Lady took
My hand in her spare hand
Jewelled and soft and grand,
And looked with a long long look
Of hunger in my face;
As if she tried to trace
Features she ought to know,
And half hoped, half feared, to find.
Whatever was in her mind
She heaved a sigh at last,
And began to talk to me.

'Your nurse was my dear nurse,
And her nursling's dear,' said she:
'No one told me a word
Of her getting worse and worse,
Till her poor life was past'
(Here my Lady's tears dropped fast):
'I might have been with her,
I might have promised and heard,
But she had no comforter.
She might have told me much
Which now I shall never know,

Never never shall know.'
She sat by me sobbing so,
And seemed so woe-begone,
That I laid one hand upon
Hers with a timid touch,
Scarce thinking what I did,
Not knowing what to say:
That moment her face was hid
In the pillow close by mine,
Her arm was flung over me,
She hugged me, sobbing so
As if her heart would break,
And kissed me where I lay.

After this she often came
To bring me fruit or wine,
Or sometimes hothouse flowers.
And at nights I lay awake
Often and often thinking
What to do for her sake.
Wet or dry it was the same:
She would come in at all hours,
Set me eating and drinking
And say I must grow strong;
At last the day seemed long
And home seemed scarcely home
If she did not come.

Well, I grew strong again:
In time of primroses,
I went to pluck them in the lane;
In time of nestling birds,
I heard them chirping round the house;
And all the herds
Were out at grass when I grew strong,
And days were waxen long,
And there was work for bees
Among the May-bush boughs,

And I had shot up tall,
And life felt after all
Pleasant, and not so long
When I grew strong.

I was going to the Hall
To be my Lady's maid:
'Her little friend,' she said to me,
'Almost her child,'
She said and smiled
Sighing painfully;
Blushing, with a second flush
As if she blushed to blush.

Friend, servant, child: just this
My standing at the Hall;
The other servants call me 'Miss,'
My Lady calls me 'Margaret,'
With her clear voice musical.
She never chides when I forget
This or that; she never chides.
Except when people come to stay,
(And that's not often) at the Hall,
I sit with her all day
And ride out when she rides.
She sings to me and makes me sing;
Sometimes I read to her,
Sometimes we merely sit and talk.
She noticed once my ring
And made me tell its history:
That evening in our garden walk
She said she should infer
The ring had been my father's first,
Then my mother's, given for me
To the nurse who nursed
My mother in her misery,
That so quite certainly

Some one might know me, who . . .
Then she was silent, and I too.

I hate when people come:
The women speak and stare
And mean to be so civil.
This one will stroke my hair,
That one will pat my cheek
And praise my Lady's kindness,
Expecting me to speak;
I like the proud ones best
Who sit as struck with blindness,
As if I wasn't there.
But if any gentleman
Is staying at the Hall
(Tho' few come prying here),
My Lady seems to fear
Some downright dreadful evil,
And makes me keep my room
As closely as she can:
So I hate when people come,
It is so troublesome.
In spite of all her care,
Sometimes to keep alive
I sometimes do contrive
To get out in the grounds
For a whiff of wholesome air,
Under the rose you know:
It's charming to break bounds,
Stolen waters are sweet,
And what's the good of feet
If for days they mustn't go?
Give me a longer tether,
Or I may break from it.

Now I have eyes and ears
And just some little wit:
'Almost my Lady's child';

I recollect she smiled,
Sighed and blushed together;
Then her story of the ring
Sounds not improbable,
She told it me so well
It seemed the actual thing: —
Oh, keep your counsel close,
But I guess under the rose,
In long past summer weather
When the world was blossoming,
And the rose upon its thorn:
I guess not who he was
Flawed honour like a glass
And made my life forlorn,
But my Mother, Mother, Mother,
Oh, I know her from all other.

My Lady, you might trust
Your daughter with your fame.
Trust me, I would not shame
Our honourable name,
For I have noble blood
Tho' I was bred in dust
And brought up in the mud.
I will not press my claim,
Just leave me where you will:
But you might trust your daughter,
For blood is thicker than water
And you're my mother still.

So my Lady holds her own
With condescending grace,
And fills her lofty place
With an untroubled face
As a queen may fill a throne.
While I could hint a tale —
(But then I am her child) —
Would make her quail;

Would set her in the dust,
Lorn with no comforter,
Her glorious hair defiled
And ashes on her cheek:
The decent world would thrust
Its finger out at her,
Not much displeased I think
To make a nine days' stir;
The decent world would sink
Its voice to speak of her.

Now this is what I mean
To do, no more, no less:
Never to speak, or show
Bare sign of what I know.
Let the blot pass unseen;
Yea, let her never guess
I hold the tangled clue
She huddles out of view.
Friend, servant, almost child,
So be it and nothing more
On this side of the grave.
Mother, in Paradise,
You'll see with clearer eyes;
Perhaps in this world even
When you are like to die
And face to face with Heaven
You'll drop for once the lie:
But you must drop the mask, not I.

My Lady promises
Two hundred pounds with me
Whenever I may wed
A man she can approve:
And since besides her bounty
I'm fairest in the county
(For so I've heard it said,
Tho' I don't vouch for this),

Her promised pounds may move
Some honest man to see
My virtues and my beauties;
Perhaps the rising grazier,
Or temperance publican,
May claim my wifely duties.
Meanwhile I wait their leisure
And grace-bestowing pleasure,
I wait the happy man;
But if I hold my head
And pitch my expectations
Just higher than their level,
They must fall back on patience:
I may not mean to wed,
Yet I'll be civil.

Now sometimes in a dream
My heart goes out of me
To build and scheme,
Till I sob after things that seem
So pleasant in a dream:
A home such as I see
My blessed neighbours live in
With father and with mother,
All proud of one another,
Named by one common name
From baby in the bud
To full-blown workman father;
It's little short of Heaven.
I'd give my gentle blood
To wash my special shame
And drown my private grudge;
I'd toil and moil much rather
The dingiest cottage drudge
Whose mother need not blush,
Than live here like a lady
And see my Mother flush
And hear her voice unsteady

Sometimes, yet never dare
Ask to share her care.

Of course the servants sneer
Behind my back at me;
Of course the village girls,
Who envy me my curls
And gowns and idleness,
Take comfort in a jeer;
Of course the ladies guess
Just so much of my history
As points the emphatic stress
With which they laud my Lady;
The gentlemen who catch
A casual glimpse of me
And turn again to see,
Their valets on the watch
To speak a word with me,
All know and sting me wild;
Till I am almost ready
To wish that I were dead,
No faces more to see,
No more words to be said,
My Mother safe at last
Disburdened of her child,
And the past past.

'All equal before God' –
Our Rector has it so,
And sundry sleepers nod:
It may be so; I know
All are not equal here,
And when the sleepers wake
They make a difference.
'All equal in the grave' –
That shows an obvious sense:
Yet something which I crave
Not death itself brings near;

How should death half atone
For all my past; or make
The name I bear my own?

I love my dear old Nurse
Who loved me without gains;
I love my mistress even,
Friend, Mother, what you will:
But I could almost curse
My Father for his pains;
And sometimes at my prayer
Kneeling in sight of Heaven
I almost curse him still:
Why did he set his snare
To catch at unaware
My Mother's foolish youth;
Load me with shame that's hers,
And her with something worse,
A lifelong lie for truth?

I think my mind is fixed
On one point and made up:
To accept my lot unmixed;
Never to drug the cup
But drink it by myself.
I'll not be wooed for pelf;
I'll not blot out my shame
With any man's good name;
But nameless as I stand,
My hand is my own hand,
And nameless as I came
I go to the dark land.

'All equal in the grave' –
I bide my time till then:
'All equal before God' –
Today I feel His rod,
Tomorrow He may save:
            Amen.

CHRISTINA ROSSETTI

John Anderson my Jo

John Anderson my jo John
I wonder what ye mean
to lie sae lang i'the mornin
and sit sae late at e'en
ye'll bleer a' your een John
and why do ye so
come sooner to your bed at een
John Anderson my jo

John Anderson my jo John
when first that ye began
ye had as good a tail tree
as ony ither man
but now its waxen wan John
and wrinkles to and fro
I've twa gae ups from ae gae down
John Anderson my jo

I'm backit like a salmon
I'm breastit like a swan
my wame it is a down cod
my middle ye may span
frae my tap knot to my tae John
I'm like the new fa'n snow
and it's a' for your convenience
John Anderson my jo

belly/pillow

O it is a fine thing
to keep out o'er the dyke
but its a meikle finer thing
buttocks/work   to see your hurdies fyke
to see your hurdies fyke John
and hit the rising blow
bagpipe   it's then I like your chanter pipe
John Anderson my jo

When ye come on before John
see that ye do your best
when ye begin to haud me
see that ye grip me fast
see that ye grip me fast John
until that I cry *oh!*
your back shall crack or I do that
John Anderson my jo

John Anderson my jo John
ye're welcome when ye please
it's either in the warm bed
bedclothes   or else aboon the claes
or ye shall hae the horns John
upon your head to grow
an that's the cuckold's mallison
John Anderson my jo

ANON

Westron Wynde

Westron wynde when wyll thow blow
the smalle rayne downe can rayne –
Cryst yf my love wer in my armys
and I yn my bed agayne!

ANON

A Last Will and Testament

To my dear wife,
My joy and life,
I freely now do give her
    My whole estate,
    With all my plate,
Being just about to leave her.

A tub of soap,
A long cart-rope,
A frying-pan and kettle;
    An ashes pail,
    A threshing flail,
An iron wedge and beetle.

Two painted chairs,
Nine warden pears,
A large old dripping platter;
    The bed of hay,
    On which I lay,
An old saucepan for butter.

A little mug,
A two-quart jug,
A bottle full of brandy;
    A looking-glass,
    To see your face,
You'll find it very handy.

A musket true
As ever flew,
A pound of shot, and wallet;
    A leather sash,
    My calabash,
My powder-horn, and bullet.

An old sword-blade,
A garden spade,
A hoe, a rake, a ladder;
    A wooden can,
    A close-stool pan,
A clyster-pipe, and bladder.

A greasy hat,
My old ram-cat,
A yard and half of linen;
    A pot of grease,
    A woollen fleece,
In order for your spinning.

A small toothcomb,
An ashen broom,
A candlestick, and hatchet;
    A coverlid,
    Striped down with red,
A bag of rags to patch it.

A ragged mat,
A tub of fat,
A book, put out by Bunyan,
    Another book,
    By Robin Rook,
A skein, or two, of spun yarn.

An old black muff,
Some garden stuff,
A quantity of borage;
    Some Devil's-weed,
    And burdock seed,
To season well your porridge.

A chafing-dish,
With one salt fish,
If I am not mistaken;
   A leg of pork,
   A broken fork,
And half a flitch of bacon.

A spinning-wheel,
One peck of meal;
A knife without a handle;
   A rusty lamp,
   Two quarts of samp,
And half a tallow candle.

coarse maize

My pouch and pipes,
Two oxen tripes,
An oaken dish well carved;
   My little dog,
   And spotted hog,
With two young pigs just starved.

This is my store,
I have no more,
I heartily do give it;
   My days are spun,
   My life is done,
And so I think to leave it.

JOHN WINSTANLEY

when i am quit forgoten

Sampler Rhymes

When i was Young
and in my Prime
here you may see
how i spent my time:

SARAH PELHAM

This is my Work so
You may see. what
care my mother as
took of me. ann bell.

ANN BELL

Elizabeth Walters is my name
in Wales is my nation
ystradveltœ is my dwelling
and Christ is my salvation
When i am dead and in my grave
an all my bones are rotten
if this you see
Remember me
when i am quit forgoten.

ELIZABETH WALTERS

Assist Me While I wander Here
    Amidre Sworld of Cares
Incline My Heart to Pray With Love
    And then Accept My Prayers.

CAROLINE CODLING

With cheerful mind we yield to Men,
The higher honours of the Pen,
  The Needle's our great Care:
In this we chiefly wish to shine,
How far the art's already mine,
  This Sampler will declare!

FRANCES GRAY

Sweet it is to be a child
Tender merciful and mild
Ever ready to perform
Acts of kindness to a worm —

TABITHA

Virtue alone Can Never die. but Lives to
    immortality
from haughty Looks Ill turn aside. &
mortifie my Pride

HANNAH TAYLOR

Place

from Crusoe in England

A new volcano has erupted,
the papers say, and last week I was reading
where some ship saw an island being born:
at first a breath of steam, ten miles away;
and then a black fleck – basalt, probably –
rose in the mate's binoculars
and caught on the horizon like a fly.
They named it. But my poor old island's still
un-rediscovered, un-renamable.
None of the books has ever got it right.

Well, I had fifty-two
miserable, small volcanoes I could climb
with a few slithery strides –
volcanoes dead as ash heaps.
I used to sit on the edge of the highest one
and count the others standing up,
naked and leaden, with their heads blown off.
I'd think that if they were the size
I thought volcanoes should be, then I had
become a giant;
and if I had become a giant,
I couldn't bear to think what size
the goats and turtles were,
or the gulls, or the overlapping rollers
– a glittering hexagon of rollers
closing and closing in, but never quite,
glittering and glittering, though the sky
was mostly overcast.

My island seemed to be
a sort of cloud-dump. All the hemisphere's
left-over clouds arrived and hung
above the craters – their parched throats
were hot to touch.
Was that why it rained so much?

And why sometimes the whole place hissed?
The turtles lumbered by, high-domed,
hissing like teakettles.
(And I'd have given years, or taken a few,
for any sort of kettle, of course.)
The folds of lava, running out to sea,
would hiss. I'd turn. And then they'd prove
to be more turtles.
The beaches were all lava, variegated,
black, red, and white, and gray;
the marbled colors made a fine display.
And I had waterspouts. Oh,
half a dozen at a time, far out,
they'd come and go, advancing and retreating,
their heads in cloud, their feet in moving patches
of scuffed-up white.
Glass chimneys, flexible, attenuated,
sacerdotal beings of glass . . . I watched
the water spiral up in them like smoke.
Beautiful, yes, but not much company.

I often gave way to self-pity.
'Do I deserve this? I suppose I must.
I wouldn't be here otherwise. Was there
a moment when I actually chose this?
I don't remember, but there could have been.'
What's wrong about self-pity, anyway?
With my legs dangling down familiarly
over a crater's edge, I told myself
'Pity should begin at home.' So the more
pity I felt, the more I felt at home.

The sun set in the sea; the same odd sun
rose from the sea,
and there was one of it and one of me.
The island had one kind of everything:
one tree snail, a bright violet-blue
with a thin shell, crept over everything,

over the one variety of tree,
a sooty, scrub affair.
Snail shells lay under these in drifts
and, at a distance,
you'd swear that they were beds of irises.
There was one kind of berry, a dark red.
I tried it, one by one, and hours apart.
Sub-acid, and not bad, no ill effects;
and so I made home-brew. I'd drink
the awful, fizzy, stinging stuff
that went straight to my head
and play my home-made flute
(I think it had the weirdest scale on earth)
and, dizzy, whoop and dance among the goats.
Home-made, home-made! But aren't we all?
I felt a deep affection for
the smallest of my island industries.
No, not exactly, since the smallest was
a miserable philosophy.

ELIZABETH BISHOP

My Orcha'd in Linden Lea

'Ithin the woodlands, flow'ry gleäded,
    By the woak tree's mossy moot,
The sheenen grass-bleädes, timber-sheäded,
    Now do quiver under voot;
An' birds do whissle over head,
An' water's bubblen in its bed,
An' there vor me the apple tree
Do leän down low in Linden Lea.

stump

When leaves that leätely wer a-springen
   Now do feäde 'ithin the copse,
An' païnted birds do hush their zingen
   Up upon the timber's tops;
An' brown-leav'd fruit's a-turnen red,
In cloudless zunsheen, over head,
Wi' fruit vor me, the apple tree
Do leän down low in Linden Lea.

Let other vo'k meäke money vaster
   In the aïr o' dark-room'd towns,
I don't dread a peevish meäster;
   Though noo man do heed my frowns,
I be free to goo abrode,
Or teäke ageän my homeward road
To where, vor me, the apple tree
Do leän down low in Linden Lea.

WILLIAM BARNES

Inversnaid

This darksome burn, horseback brown,
His rollrock highroad roaring down,
In coop and in comb the fleece of his foam
Flutes and low to the lake falls home.

A windpuff-bonnet of fáwn-fróth
Turns and twindles over the broth
Of a pool so pitchblack, féll-frówning,
It rounds and rounds Despair to drowning.

misted   Degged with dew, dappled with dew
Are the groins of the braes that the brook treads
   through,
Wiry heathpacks, flitches of fern,
And the beadbonny ash that sits over the burn.

What would the world be, once bereft
Of wet and of wildness? Let them be left,
O let them be left, wildness and wet;
Long live the weeds and the wilderness yet.

GERARD MANLEY HOPKINS

Preston

Proud Preston poor people
fine church and no steeple

ANON

Utah

Somewhere nowhere in Utah, a boy by the
    roadside,
gun in his hand, and the rare dumb hard tears
    flowing.
Beside him, the greyheaded man has let one arm
    slide
awkwardly over his shoulder, is talking and
    pointing
at whatever it is, dead, in the dust on the ground.

By the old parked Chevy, two women, talking
    and watching.
Their skirts flag forward. Bandannas twist with
    their hair.
Around them some sheep and a fence and the
    sagebrush burning
and burning with its blue flame. In the distance,
    where
the mountains are clouds, lightning, but no rain.

ANNE STEVENSON

The Lament of Swordy Well

Petitioners are full of prayers
To fall in pitys way
But if her hand the gift forbears
Theyll sooner swear then pray
They're not the worst to want who lurch
On plenty with complaints
No more then those who go to church
Are eer the better saints

I hold no hat to beg a mite
Nor pick it up when thrown
Nor limping leg I hold in sight
But pray to keep my own
Where profit gets his clutches in
Theres little he will leave
Gain stooping for a single pin
Will stick it on his sleeve

For passers bye I never pin
No troubles to my breast
Nor carry round some names
More money from the rest
Im swordy well a piece of land
Thats fell upon the town
Who worked me till I couldnt stand
And crush me now Im down

In parish bonds I well may wail
Reduced to every shift
Pity may grieve at troubles tale
But cunning shares the gift
Harvests with plenty on his brow
Leaves losses taunts with me
Yet gain comes yearly with the plough
And will not let me be

Alas dependance thou'rt a brute
Want only understands
His feelings wither branch and root
That falls in parish hands
The muck that clouts the ploughmans shoe
The moss that hides the stone
Now Im become the parish due
Is more then I can own

Though Im no man yet any wrong
Some sort of right may seek
And I am glad if een a song
Gives me the room to speak
Ive got among such grubbling geer
And such a hungry pack
If I brought harvests twice a year
They'd bring me nothing back

When war their tyrant prices got
I trembled with alarms
They fell and saved my little spot
Or towns had turned to farms
Let profit keep an humble place
That gentry may be known
Let pedigrees their honours trace
And toil enjoy its own

The silver springs grown naked dykes
Scarce own a bunch of rushes
When grain got high the tasteless tykes
Grubbed up trees banks and bushes
And me they turned me inside out
For sand and grit and stones
And turned my old green hills about
And pickt my very bones

These things that claim my own as theirs
Where born but yesterday
But ere I fell to town affairs
I were as proud as they
I kept my horses cows and sheep
And built the town below
Ere they had cat or dog to keep
And then to use me so

Parish allowance gaunt and dread
Had it the earth to keep
Would even pine the bees to dead
To save an extra keep
Prides workhouse is a place that yields
From poverty its gains
And mines a workhouse for the fields
A starving the remains

The bees flye round in feeble rings
And find no blossom bye
Then thrum their almost weary wings
Upon the moss and die
Rabbits that find my hills turned oer
Forsake my poor abode
They dread a workhouse like the poor
And nibble on the road

If with a clover bottle now
Spring dares to lift her head
The next day brings the hasty plough
And makes me miserys bed
The butterflyes may wir and come
I cannot keep em now
Nor can they bear my parish home
That withers on my brow

No now not een a stone can lie
Im just what eer they like
My hedges like the winter flye
And leave me but the dyke
My gates are thrown from off the hooks
The parish thoroughfare
Lord he thats in the parish books
Has little wealth to spare

I couldnt keep a dust of grit
Nor scarce a grain of sand
But bags and carts claimed every bit
And now theyve got the land
I used to bring the summers life
To many a butterflye
But in oppressions iron strife
Dead tussocks bow and sigh

Ive scarce a nook to call my own
For things that creep or flye
The beetle hiding neath a stone
Does well to hurry bye
Stock eats my struggles every day
As bare as any road
He's sure to be in somthings way
If eer he stirs abroad

I am no man to whine and beg
But fond of freedom still
I hing no lies on pitys peg
To bring a gris to mill
On pitys back I neednt jump
My looks speak loud alone
My only tree they've left a stump
And nought remains my own

My mossy hills gains greedy hand
And more then greedy mind
Levels into a russet land
Nor leaves a bent behind
In summers gone I bloomed in pride
Folks came for miles to prize
My flowers that bloomed no where beside
And scarce believed their eyes

Yet worried with a greedy pack
They rend and delve and tear
The very grass from off my back
Ive scarce a rag to wear
Gain takes my freedom all away
Since its dull suit I wore
And yet scorn vows I never pay
And hurts me more and more

And should the price of grain get high
Lord help and keep it low
I shant possess a single flye
Or get a weed to grow
I shant possess a yard of ground
To bid a mouse to thrive
For gain has put me in a pound
I scarce can keep alive

I own Im poor like many more
But then the poor mun live
And many came for miles before
For what I had to give
But since I fell upon the town
They pass me with a sigh
Ive scarce the room to say sit down
And so they wander bye

Though now I seem so full of clack
Yet when yer' riding bye
The very birds upon my back
Are not more fain to flye
I feel so lorn in this disgrace
God send the grain to fall
I am the oldest in the place
And the worst served of all

Lord bless ye I was kind to all
And poverty in me
Could always find a humble stall
A rest and lodging free
Poor bodys with an hungry ass
I welcomed many a day
And gave him tether room and grass
And never said him nay

There was a time my bit of ground
Made freemen of the slave
impounder   The ass no pindard dare to pound
When I his supper gave
The gipseys camp was not affraid
I made his dwelling free
Till vile enclosure came and made
A parish slave of me

The gipseys further on sojourn
No parish bounds they like
No sticks I own and would earth burn
I shouldnt own a dyke
I am no friend to lawless work
Nor would a rebel be
And why I call a christian turk
Is they are turks to me

And if I could but find a friend
With no deciet to sham
Who'd send me some few sheep to tend
And leave me as I am
To keep my hills from cart and plough
And strife of mongerel men
And as spring found me find me now
I should look up agen

And save his Lordships woods that past
The day of danger dwell
Of all the fields I am the last
That my own face can tell
Yet what with stone pits delving holes
And strife to buy and sell
My name will quickly be the whole
Thats left of swordy well

JOHN CLARE

from Sainte Lucie

single-stalked	Pomme arac,
	otaheite apple,
	pomme cythere,
pomegranate	pomme granate,
	moubain,
pineapple	z'ananas
	the pine apple's
	Aztec helmet,
	pomme,
	I have forgotten
	what pomme for
	the Irish potato,
	cerise,
	the cherry,
	z'aman
	sea-almonds
	by the crisp
	sea-bursts,
	au bord de la 'ouviere.
	Come back to me
	my language.
	Come back,
cocoa	cacao,
amulet	grigri,
thrush	solitaire,
scissor	ciseau
	the scissor-bird
	no nightingales
	except, once,
	in the indigo mountains
	of Jamaica, blue depth,
	deep as coffee,
	flicker of pimento,

the shaft light
on a yellow ackee
the bark alone bare

jardins
en montagnes
en haut betassion
the wet leather reek
of the hill donkey

evening opens at
a text of fireflies,
in the mountain huts
ti cailles betassion
candles,
candleflies
the black night bending
cups in its hard palms
cool thin water
this is important water,
important?
imported?
water is important
also very important
the red rust drum
the evening deep
as coffee
the morning powerful
important coffee
the villages shut
all day in the sun.

In the empty schoolyard
teacher dead today
the fruit rotting
yellow on the ground,
dyes from Gauguin
the pomme arac dyes

the earth purple,
the ochre roads
still waiting in the sun
for my shadow,
O so you is Walcott?
you is Roddy brother?
Teacher Alix son?
and the small rivers
with important names.

And the important corporal
in the country station
en betassion
looking towards the thick
green slopes of cocoa
the sun that melts
the asphalt at noon,
and the woman in the shade
of the breadfruit bent over
the lip of the valley,
below her, blue-green
the lost, lost valleys
of sugar, the bus-rides,
the fields of bananas
the tanker still rusts
in the lagoon at Roseau,
and around what corner

was uttered a single
yellow leaf,
from the frangipani
a tough bark, reticent,
but when it flowers
delivers hard lilies,
pungent, recalling
Martina, or Eunice
or Lucilla,
who comes down the steps

with the cool, side flow
as spring water eases
over shelves of rock
in some green ferny hole
by the road in the mountains,
her smile like the whole country
her smell, earth,
red-brown earth, her armpits
a reaping, her arms
saplings, an old woman
that she is now,
with other generations
of daughters flowing
down the steps,
gens betassion,
belle ti fille betassion,
until their teeth go,
and all the rest,

O Martinas, Lucillas,
I'm a wild golden apple
that will burst with love,
of you and your men,
those I never told enough
with my young poet's eyes
crazy with the country,
generations going,
generations gone,
moi c'est gens St Lucie.
C'est la moi sorti;
is there that I born.

DEREK WALCOTT

from Don Juan

Don Juan had got out on Shooter's Hill,
    Sunset the time, the place the same declivity
Which looks along that vale of good and ill,
    Where London streets ferment in full activity,
While everything around was calm and still,
    Except the creak of wheels, which on their
                                        pivot he
Heard, and that bee-like, bubbling, busy hum
Of cities, that boils over with their scum.

I say, Don Juan, wrapt in contemplation,
    Walked on behind his carriage o'er the
                                        summit,
And lost in wonder of so great a nation,
    Gave way to't, since he could not overcome it.
'And here,' he cried, 'is Freedom's chosen station.
    Here peals the people's voice, nor can entomb
                                                it
Racks, prisons, inquisitions. Resurrection
Awaits it, each new meeting or election.

'Here are chaste wives, pure lives. Here people
                                        pay
    But what they please, and if that things be
                                        dear,
'Tis only that they love to throw away
    Their cash, to show how much they have a
                                        year.
Here laws are all inviolate; none lay
    Traps for the traveller; every highway's clear.
Here' – he was interrupted by a knife,
With 'Damn your eyes! your money or your life!'

These freeborn sounds proceeded from four pads
   In ambush laid, who had perceived him loiter
Behind his carriage and like handy lads
   Had seized the lucky hour to reconnoitre,
In which the heedless gentleman who gads
   Upon the road, unless he prove a fighter,
May find himself within that isle of riches
Exposed to lose his life as well as breeches.

Juan, who did not understand a word
   Of English, save their shibboleth 'God damn!'
And even that he had so rarely heard,
   He sometimes thought 'twas only their
   'salaam'
Or 'God be with you!' – and 'tis not absurd
   To think so, for half English as I am
(To my misfortune) never can I say
I heard them wish 'God with you,' save that way –

Juan yet quickly understood their gesture
   And being somewhat choleric and sudden,
Drew forth a pocket pistol from his vesture
   And fired it into one assailant's pudding,
Who fell, as rolls an ox o'er in his pasture,
   And roared out, as he writhed his native mud
                         in,
Unto his nearest follower or henchman,
'Oh Jack! I'm floored by that 'ere bloody
   Frenchman!'

On which Jack and his train set off at speed,
    And Juan's suite, late scattered at a distance,
Came up, all marvelling at such a deed
    And offering as usual late assistance.
Juan, who saw the moon's late minion bleed
    As if his veins would pour out his existence,
Stood calling out for bandages and lint
And wished he had been less hasty with his flint.

'Perhaps,' thought he, 'it is the country's wont
    To welcome foreigners in this way. Now
I recollect some innkeepers who don't
    Differ, except in robbing with a bow,
In lieu of a bare blade and brazen front.
    But what is to be done? I can't allow
The fellow to lie groaning on the road.
So take him up; I'll help you with the load.'

But ere they could perform this pious duty,
    The dying man cried, 'Hold! I've got my gruel!
gin Oh for a glass of max! We've missed our booty.
    Let me die where I am!' And as the fuel
Of life shrunk in his heart, and thick and sooty
    The drops fell from his death-wound, and he
        drew ill
His breath, he from his swelling throat untied
A kerchief, crying 'Give Sal that!' and died.

The cravat stained with bloody drops fell down
    Before Don Juan's feet. He could not tell
Exactly why it was before him thrown,
    Nor what the meaning of the man's farewell.
thief Poor Tom was once a kiddy upon town,
sporting amateur   A thorough varmint and a real swell,
affected/sporting Full flash, all fancy, until fairly diddled,
His pockets first and then his body riddled.

Don Juan, having done the best he could
   In all the circumstances of the case,
A soon as 'crowner's 'quest' allowed, pursued
   His travels to the capital apace,
Esteeming it a little hard he should
   In twelve hours' time and very little space
Have been obliged to slay a freeborn native
In self-defence. This made him meditative.

He from the world had cut off a great man,
   Who in his time had made heroic bustle.
Who in a row like Tom could lead the van,
safe house / playhouse   Booze in the ken or at the spellken hustle?
confound a gull   Who queer a flat? Who (spite of Bow Street's
                              ban)
robbery on horseback   On the high toby spice so flash the muzzle?
spree / trull Who on a lark with black-eyed Sal (his blowing)
So prime, so swell, so nutty, and so knowing?

But Tom's no more, and so no more of Tom.
   Heroes must die; and by God's blessing 'tis
Not long before the most of them go home.
   Hail, Thamis, hail! Upon thy verge it is
That Juan's chariot, rolling like a drum
   In thunder, holds the way it can't well miss,
Through Kennington and all the other 'tons',
Which make us wish ourselves in town at once.

GEORGE GORDON, LORD BYRON

Broagh

strips of land	Riverbank, the long rigs
dock leaves	ending in broad docken
path	and a canopied pad
	down to the ford.
soil	The garden mould
	bruised easily, the shower
	gathering in your heelmark
	was the black O
	in *Broagh*,
	its low tattoo
elder trees	among the windy boortrees
	and rhubarb-blades
	ended almost
	suddenly, like that last
	gh the strangers found
	difficult to manage.

SEAMUS HEANEY

Our Village – by a Villager

'Sweet Auburn, loveliest village of the plain' – Goldsmith

Our village, that's to say not Miss Mitford's
    village, but our village of Bullock Smithy,
Is come into by an avenue of trees, three oak
    pollards, two elders, and a withy;
And in the middle, there's a green of about not
    exceeding an acre and a half;

It's common to all, and fed off by nineteen cows,
    six ponies, three horses, five asses, two foals,
    seven pigs, and a calf!
Besides a pond in the middle, as is held by a
    similar sort of common law lease,
And contains twenty ducks, six drakes, three
    ganders, two dead dogs, four drowned kittens,
    and twelve geese.
Of course the green's cropt very close, and does
    famous for bowling when the little village boys
    play at cricket;
Only some horse, or pig, or cow, or great
    jackass, is sure to come and stand right before
    the wicket.
There's fifty-five private houses, let alone barns
    and workshops, and pigstyes, and poultry huts,
    and such-like sheds;
With plenty of public-houses – two Foxes, one
    Green Man, three Bunch of Grapes, one
    Crown, and six King's Heads.
The Green Man is reckoned the best, as the only
    one that for love or money can raise
A postilion, a blue jacket, two deplorable lame
    white horses, and a ramshackled 'neat
    postchaise'.
There's one parish church for all the people,
    whatsoever may be their ranks in life or their
    degrees,
Except one very damp, small, dark, freezing cold,
    little Methodist chapel of ease;
And close by the churchyard there's a
    stonemason's yard, that when the time is
    seasonable
Will furnish with afflictions sore and marble urns
    and cherubims very low and reasonable.
There's a cage, comfortable enough; I've been in
    it with old Jack Jeffrey and Tom Pike;

For the Green Man next door will send you in
    ale, gin or anything else you like.
I can't speak of the stocks, as nothing remains of
    them but the upright post;
But the pound is kept in repairs for the sake of
    Cob's horse, as is always there almost.
There's a smithy of course, where that queer sort
    of a chap in his way, Old Joe Bradley,
Perpetually hammers and stammers, for he
    stutters and shoes horses very badly.
There's a shop of all sorts, that sells everything,
    kept by the widow of Mr Task;
But when you go there it's ten to one she's out of
    every thing you ask.
You'll know her house by the swarm of boys,
    like flies, about the old sugary cask:
There are six empty houses, and not so well
    papered inside as out,
For billstickers won't beware, but sticks notices
    of sales and election placards all about.
That's the Doctor's with a green door, where the
    garden pots in the windows is seen;
A weakly monthly rose that don't blow, and a
    dead geranium, and a tea-plant with five black
    leaves and one green.
As for hollyoaks at the cottage doors, and
    honeysuckles and jasmines, you may go and
    whistle;
But the Tailor's front garden grows two
    cabbages, a dock, a ha'porth of pennyroyal,
    two dandelions, and a thistle.
There are three small orchards – Mr Busby's the
    schoolmaster's is the chief –
With two pear-trees that don't bear; one plum
    and an apple, that every year is stripped by a
    thief.
There's another small day-school too, kept by the
    respectable Mrs Gaby.

A select establishment, for six little boys and one
    big, and four little girls and a baby;
There's a rectory, with pointed gables and
    strange odd chimneys that never smokes,
For the rector don't live on his living like other
    Christian sort of folks;
There's a barber's, once a week well filled with
    rough black-bearded, shock-headed churls.
And a window with two feminine men's heads,
    and two masculine ladies in false curls;
There's a butcher's, and a carpenter's, and a
    plumber's, and a small greengrocer's, and a
    baker,
But he won't bake on a Sunday, and there's a
    sexton that's a coal-merchant besides, and an
    undertaker;
And a toy-shop, but not a whole one, for a
    village can't compare with the London shops;
One window sells drums, dolls, kites, carts, bats,
    Clout's balls, and the other sells malt and
    hops.
And Mrs Brown, in domestic economy not to be
    a bit behind her betters,
Lets her house to a milliner, a watchmaker, a rat-
    catcher, a cobbler, lives in it herself, and it's
    the post-office for letters.
Now I've gone through all the village – ay, from
    end to end, save and except one more house,
But I haven't come to that – and I hope I never
    shall – and that's the Village Poor House!

THOMAS HOOD

A Removal from Terry Street

On a squeaking cart, they push the usual stuff,
A mattress, bed ends, cups, carpets, chairs,
Four paperback westerns. Two whistling youths
In surplus US Army battle-jackets
Remove their sister's goods. Her husband
Follows, carrying on his shoulders the son
Whose mischief we are glad to see removed,
And pushing, of all things, a lawnmower.
There is no grass in Terry Street. The worms
Come up cracks in concrete yards in moonlight.
That man, I wish him well. I wish him grass.

DOUGLAS DUNN

Murder

from The Ring and the Book

Do you see this square old yellow Book, I toss
I' the air, and catch again, and twirl about
By the crumpled vellum covers, — pure crude fact
Secreted from a man's life when hearts beat hard,
And brains, high-blooded, ticked two centuries
    since?
Examine it yourselves! I found this book,
Gave a *lira* for it, eightpence English just,
(Mark the predestination!) when a Hand,
Always above my shoulder, pushed me once,
One day still fierce 'mid many a day struck calm,
Across a Square in Florence, crammed with
    booths,
Buzzing and blaze, noontide and market-time;
Toward Baccio's marble, — ay, the basement-
    ledge
O' the pedestal where sits and menaces
John of the Black Bands with the upright spear,
'Twixt palace and church, — Riccardi where they
    lived,
His race, and San Lorenzo where they lie.
This book, — precisely on that palace-step
Which, meant for lounging knaves o' the Medici,
Now serves re-venders to display their ware, —
'Mongst odds and ends of ravage, picture-frames
White through the worn gilt, mirror-sconces
    chipped,
Bronze angel-heads once knobs attached to
    chests,
(Handled when ancient dames chose forth
    brocade)
Modern chalk drawings, studies from the nude,
Samples of stone, jet, breccia, porphyry
Polished and rough, sundry amazing busts
In baked earth, (broken, Providence be praised!)

A wreck of tapestry, proudly-purposed web
When reds and blues were indeed red and blue,
Now offered as a mat to save bare feet
(Since carpets constitute a cruel cost)
inlaid stone floor   Treading the chill scagliola bedward: then
halfpence   A pile of brown-etched prints, two *crazie* each,
Stopped by a conch a-top from fluttering forth
— Sowing the Square with works of one and the
     same
Master, the imaginative Sienese
Great in the scenic backgrounds — (name and
     fame
None of you know, nor does he fare the worse:)
From these . . . Oh, with a Lionard going cheap
If it should prove, as promised, that Joconde
Whereof a copy contents the Louvre! — these
I picked this book from. Five compeers in flank
Stood left and right of it as tempting more —
A dogseared Spicilegium, the fond tale
O' the Frail One of the Flower, by young Dumas,
Vulgarized Horace for the use of schools,
The Life, Death, Miracles of Saint Somebody,
Saint Somebody Else, his Miracles, Death and
     Life, —
With this, one glance at the lettered back of
     which,
And 'Stall!' cried I: a *lira* made it mine.

ROBERT BROWNING

Lizie Wan

house   Lizie Wan sits at her father's bower door
weeping and making a mane
and by there came her father dear
what ails thee Lizie Wan?

I ail and I ail dear father she said
and I'll tell you a reason for why
there is a child between my twa sides
between my dear billy and I

brother

now Lizie Wan sits at her father's bower door
sighing and making a mane
and by there came her brother dear
what ails thee Lizie Wan

I ail I ail dear brither she said
and I'll tell you a reason for why
there is a child between my twa sides
between you dear billy and I

and hast thou tald father and mother o that?
and has thou tald sae o me?
and he has drawn his gude braid sword
that hang down by his knee

and he has cutted aff Lizie Wan's head
and her fair body in three

room

and he's awa to his mother's bower
and sair aghast was he

what ails thee what ails thee Geordy Wan
what ails thee sae fast to rin?
for I see by thy ill colour

wicked

some fallow's deed thou hast done

some fallow's deed I have done mother
and I pray you pardon me
for I've cutted aff my greyhound's head
he wadna rin for me

thy greyhound's bluid was never sae red
O my son Geordy Wan
for I see by thy ill colour
some fallow's deed thou hast done

some fallow's deed I hae done mother
and I pray you pardon me
for I hae cutted aff Lizie Wan's head
and her fair body in three

O what wilt thou do when thy father comes
    hame
O my son Geordy Wan?
I'll set my foot in a bottomless boat

sea bottom   and swim to the sea groun

and when wilt thou come hame again
O my son Geordy Wan?
the sun and the moon shall dance on the green
that night when I come hame

ANON

from The Ballad of the Yorkshire Ripper

Ower t'ills o Bingley
stormclouds clap an drain,
like opened blood-black blisters
leakin puss an pain.

Ail teems down like stair-rods,
an swells canals an becks,
an fills up studmarked goalmouths,
an bursts on mind like sex.

Cos sex is like a stormclap,
a swellin in thi cells,
when lightnin arrers through thi
an tha knows there in't owt else.

Ah've felt it in misen, like,
ikin ome part-fresh
ower limestone outcrops
like knuckles white through flesh:

ow men clap down on women
t'old em there for good
an soak up all their softness
thrash   an lounder em wi blood.

It's then I think on t'Ripper
an what e did an why,
an ow mi mates ate women,
an ow Pete med em die.

I love em for misen, like,
their skimmerin lips an eyes,
crane-flies   their ankles light as jinnyspins,
teasing   their seggy whisps an sighs,

their braided locks like catkins,
flashy   an t'curlies glashy black,
the peepin o their linnet tongues,
their way o cheekin back.

An ah look on em as equals.
But mates all say they're not,
upper hand   that men must have t'owerance
or world will go to rot.

Lad-desperate   Lad-loupin molls an gadabouts,
fellow-fond an sly,
whores/slatterns   flappy-skets an drabbletails
oo'll bleed a bloke bone-dry:

that's ow I ear em spoke of
when lads are on their tod,
an ow tha's got to leather em
to stop em gi'in t'nod.

An some o t'same in Bible
where Paul screams fit to bust
ow men are fallen creatures
but womenfolk are t'wust.

Now I reckon this fired Peter,
an men-talk were is goad,

bellowing   an culprit were our belderin God
an is ancient, bullyin road.

No, Pete weren't drove by vengeance,
madness   rountwistedness or ale,
beefy   but to show isen a baufy man –
but let me tell thi tale

       *

Peter worked in a graveyard,
diggin bone an sod.
From t'grave of a Pole, Zapolski,
e eard – e reckoned – God,

sayin: 'Lad, tha's on a mission,
ah've picked thi out o t'ruck.
Go an rip up prostitutes.
They're nobbut worms an muck.

'Streets are runnin sewers.
Streets are open sores.
Get in there wi thi scalpel
an wipe away all t'oors.'

Pete were pumped like a primus.
E felt is cravin whet.
E started cruisin Chapeltown
but e didn't kill, not yet.

E took a job on t'lorries,
a Transcontinental Ford.
E felt reet good in t'cabin.
E felt like a bloody Lord.

spoilt child

E'd bin a bit of a mardy,
angin on t'old dear's skirt.
E didn't like folks shoutin,
or scraps wi lads, or dirt.

E'd watch his dad trough offal –
trotters, liver, tripe –
or pigeon scraped from t'by-pass,
or rabbit, ung an ripe,

dirty kid

an all e'd felt were babbyish,
a fustilugs, alf-nowt,
an wished e were is younger kid
tekkin lasses out.

But now e'd started truckin
an ropin up is load
an bought isen a Bullworker
e swelled up like a toad,

an stuck is ead in motors
an messed wi carbs an ubs,
an drove wi mates to Manningham
an other arse-end pubs,

or sometimes off to Blackpool
to t'Tower or lights or pier,
or waxworks Chamber of Orrors –
aye, Pete were allus theer.

E met a lass called Sonia,
a nervy type, a shrew,
oo mithered im an nattered,
but Pete, e thought she'd do.

She seemed a cut above im,
a teacher, arty too,
oo wanted summat more'n kids.
Aye, Pete, e thought she'd do.

Cos Sonia, she weren't mucky,
not like yon other bags,
them tarts in fishnet stockins,
whores   them goers, buers, slags.

BLAKE MORRISON

Hickamore Hackamore

Riddles

A riddle a riddle as I suppose
a hundred eyes and never a nose

(potato)

Riddlum riddlum ranty pole
half arse and no hole

(ham of a hog)

Long slick black feller
pull his tail an make him beller

(gun)

Hickamore hackamore
hung on a kitchen door
nothing so long and nothing so strong
as hickamore hackamore
hung on the kitchen door

(sun)

High as the sky it flies
over the sea it ranges
still it sees no mortal rise
still it often changes

(wind)

White bird featherless
flew from paradise
perched upon the castle wall
up came Lord John landless
took it up handless
and rode away horseless
to the king's white hall

                    (snow)

A hopper o'ditches
a cropper o'corn
a wee brown cow
and a paira leather horns!

                    (hare)

White sheep white sheep on a blue hill
when the wind stops you all stand still
when the wind blows you run away slow
white sheep white sheep where do you go?

                    (to bed)

As I went down that yella bank
I met a thing all rough and rank
two great lips and a hairy beard
darn the thing it made me afeard

                    (hog)

Wooden belly iron back
fire in th'hole goes off with a crack

                    (rifle)

The cuckoo and the gowk
the laverock and the lark
the twiresnipe the weatherbleak
how many birds is that?

(three)

The land was white
the seed was black
it'll take a good scholar
to riddle me that

(paper and writing)

mouth

Black'm saut'm rough'm glower'm saw
click'm gatt'm flang'm into girnigaw

(eating a sloe)

Round the house and round the house
and there lies a white glove in the window

(snow)

round the house and round the house
and there lies a black glove in the window

(rain)

Little trotty hetty coat
in a long petticoat
and a red nose
the longer she stands
the shorter she grows

(candle)

Chip chip cherry
there isn't a man in Derry
can catch chip chip cherry

(smoke)

As I went through a guttery gap
I met a wee man with a red cap
a stick in his stern a stone in his belly
riddle me that and I'll give you a penny

(a haw)

As I went through yon guttery gap
I met my Uncle Davy
I cut off his head and drunk his blood
and left his body aisy

(bottle of whisky)

ANON

Politiks

Freedom A Come Oh!

Talla by li oh
freedom a come oh!
talla by li oh
here we dig   here we hoe

talla by li oh
slavery a gone oh!
talla by li oh
here we dig   here we hoe

talla by li oh
King George he a go
talla by li oh
here we dig   here we hoe

talla by li oh
we nuh wuk no more!
talla by li oh
here we dig   here we hoe

talla by li oh
massa he a go
talla by li oh
here we dig   here we hoe

talla by li oh
freedom a come oh!
talla by li oh
here we dig   here we sow!

ANON

Independance

Independance wid a vengeance!
Independance raisin Cain!
Jamaica start grow beard, ah hope
We chin can stan de strain!

dog thin

When daag marga him head big, an
When puss hungry him nose clean;
But every puss an daag no know
What Independance mean.

proud

Mattie seh it mean we facety,
Stan up pon we dignity,
An we doan allow nobody
Fe tek liberty wid we.

Independance is we nature
Born an bred in all we do,
An she glad fe see dat Government
Tun independant too.

She hope dem caution worl-map
Fe stop draw Jamaica small,
For de lickle speck cyaan show
We independantness at all!

Moresomever we must tell map dat
We doan like we position –
Please kindly tek we out a sea
An draw we in de ocean.

tribulation

lack of sophistication

What a crosses! Independance
Woulda never have a chance
Wid so much boogooyagga
Dah expose dem ignorance.

Daag wag im tail fe suit im size
An match im stamina –
Jamaica people need a
Independance formula!

No easy-come-by freeness tings,
Nuff labour, some privation,
Not much of dis an less of dat
An plenty studiration.

Independance wid a vengeance!
Wonder how we gwine to cope?
Jamaica start smoke pipe, ah hope
tobacco   We got nuff jackass rope!

LOUISE BENNETT

'Zion me wan go home'

Zion me wan go home
Zion me wan go home
oh oh
Zion me wan go home

Africa me wan fe go
Africa me wan fe go
oh oh
Africa me wan fe go

Tek me back to Etiopia lan
tek me back to Etiopia lan
oh oh
tek me back to Etiopia lan

Etiopia lan me faders home
Etiopia lan me faders home
oh oh
Etiopia lan me faders home

Zion me wan go home
Zion me wan go home
oh oh
Zion me wan go home

ANON

The Patriot

I am standing for peace and non-violence.
Why world is fighting fighting
Why all people of world
Are not following Mahatma Gandhi,
I am simply not understanding.
Ancient Indian Wisdom is 100% correct.
I should say even 200% correct.
But Modern generation is neglecting –
Too much going for fashion and foreign thing.

Other day I'm reading in newspaper
(Every day I'm reading Times of India
To improve my English Language)

dirty

How one goonda fellow
Throw stone at Indirabehn.
Must be student unrest fellow, I am thinking.
Friends, Romans, Countrymen, I am saying (to
    myself)
Lend me the ears.
Everything is coming –
Regeneration, Remuneration, Contraception.
Be patiently, brothers and sisters.

buttermilk

You want one glass lassi?
Very good for digestion.
With little salt lovely drink,
Better than wine;
Not that I am ever tasting the wine.
I'm the total teetotaller, completely total.
But I say
Wine is for the drunkards only.

What you think of prospects of world peace?
Pakistan behaving like this,
China behaving like that,
It is making me very sad, I am telling you.
Really, most harassing me.
All men are brothers, no?
In India also
Gujaraties, Maharashtrians, Hindiwallahs
All brothers —
Though some are having funny habits.
Still, you tolerate me,
I tolerate you,
One day Ram Rajya is surely coming.

You are going?
But you will visit again
Any time, any day,
I am not believing in ceremony.
Always I am enjoying your company.

NISSIM EZEKIEL

'Over the fence'

Over the fence –
Strawberries – grow –
Over the fence –
I could climb – if I tried, I know –
Berries are nice!

But – if I stained my Apron –
God would certainly scold!
Oh, dear, – I guess if He were a Boy –
He'd – climb – if He could!

EMILY DICKINSON

Ireland's Freedom

'What brings that currach out?' asks Séamaisín.

'It is Séan Eoghain taking a bullock across. There's another man with him going out for flour,' answers Séamas. 'The currachs had no fish today and I suppose the fish will be asleep for a while now. It was never caught so late in the year, night after night, to my knowledge.'

'Is there any talk about the freedom of Ireland, Diarmaid,' asks Séamas, 'or where is Ireland's envoy[1] these days? Is he still in America?'

'The schoolmaster says he is, travelling from place to place. He is in California now,' Diarmaid Bán answers. 'The biggest wonder is the amount of money collected for him.'

'The money is a great boon,' declares Séamaisín. 'It will be a help for somebody.'

'It is for the freedom of Ireland,' says Diarmaid.

[1] Éamonn de Valera.

'That same freedom has me deafened and I don't know what it means,' says Séamaisín.

'We to have our own King here and the connection with England to be broken,' Diarmaid answers.

'I understand now,' says Séamaisín. 'One crowned King of England and another crowned King of Ireland – that's something you'll never see, Diarmaid, so long as the sun is in the sky. If there is a crown on a King in Ireland it will be England's crown he will have to wear.'

'I hope you're proved wrong!' says Diarmaid Bán.

November 1919

TOMÁS O'CROHAN

Hamlet

As usual, the clock in the Clock bar was a good
    few minutes fast,
A fiction no one really bothered to maintain,
    unlike the story
The comrade on my left was telling, which no
    one knew for certain truth:
Back in 1922, a sergeant, I forget his name, was
    shot outside the National Bank . . .
Ah yes, what year was it that they knocked it
    down? Yet, its memory's as fresh
As the inky smell of new pound notes – which
    interferes with the beer-and-whiskey
Tang of now, like two dogs meeting in the
    revolutionary 69 of a long sniff,
Or cattle jostling shit-stained flanks in the Pound.
    For *pound*, as some wag

Interrupted, was an off-shoot of the Falls Road,
    from the Irish, *fál*, a hedge;
Hence, *any kind of enclosed thing*, its twigs and
    branches commemorated
By the soldiers' drab and olive camouflage, as
    they try to melt
Into a brick wall; red coats might be better, after
    all. *At any rate,*
This sergeant's number came up; not a winning
    one. The bullet had his name on it.
Though Sergeant X, as we'll call him, doesn't
    really feature in the story:
The nub of it is *this tin can which was heard that*
    night, trundling down
From the bank, down Balaklava Street. Which
    thousands heard, and no one ever
Saw. Which was heard for years, any night that
    trouble might be
Round the corner . . . and when it skittered to a
    halt, you knew
That someone else had snuffed it: a name drifting
    like an afterthought,
A scribbled wisp of smoke you try and grasp, as
    it becomes diminuendo, then
Vanishes. For *fál* is also *frontier, boundary*, as in
    the undiscovered country
From whose bourne no traveller returns, the
    illegible, thorny hedge of time itself –
Heartstopping moments, measured not by the
    pulse of a wrist-watch, nor
The archaic anarchists' alarm-clock, but a
    mercury tilt device
Which 'only connects' on any given bump on the
    road. So, by this winged messenger
The promise 'to pay the bearer' is fulfilled:
As someone buys another round, an Allied Irish
    Banks £10 note drowns in

The slops of the counter; a Guinness stain
  blooms on the artist's impression
Of the sinking of the *Girona*; a tiny foam hisses
  round the salamander brooch
Dredged up to show how love and money
  endure, beyond death and the Armada,
Like the bomb-disposal expert in his suit of
  salamander-cloth.
Shielded against the blast of time by a strangely
  medieval visor,
He's been outmoded by this jerky robot whose
  various attachments include
A large hook for turning over corpses that may
  be booby-trapped;
But I still have this picture of his hands held up
  to avert the future
In a final act of no surrender, as, twisting
  through the murky fathoms
Of what might have been, he is washed ashore as
  pearl and coral.

This *strange eruption to our state* is seen in other
  versions of the Falls:
A no-go area, a ghetto, a demolition zone. For
  the ghost, as it turns out –
All this according to your man, and I can well
  believe it – this tin ghost,
Since the streets it haunted were abolished, was
  never heard again.
The sleeve of Raglan Street has been unravelled;
  the helmet of Balaklava
Is torn away from the mouth. The dim glow of
  Garnet has gone out,
And with it, all but the memory of where I lived.
  I, too, heard the ghost:
A roulette trickle, or the hesitant annunciation of
  a downpour, ricocheting

Off the window; a goods train, maybe, shunting
    distantly into a siding,
Then groaning to a halt; the rainy cries of
    children after dusk.
For the voice from the grave reverberates in
    others' mouths, as the sails
Of the whitethorn hedge swell up in a little
    breeze, and tremble
Like the spiral blossom of Andromeda: so
    suddenly are shrouds and branches
Hung with street-lights, celebrating all that's lost,
    as fields are reclaimed
By the Starry Plough. So we name the
    constellations, to put a shape
On what was there; so, the storyteller picks his
    way between the isolated stars.
But, *was it really like that?* and, *is the story true?*
You might as well tear off the iron mask, and
    find that no one, after all,
Is there: nothing but a cry, a summons, clanking
    out from the smoke
Of demolition. Like some one looking for his
    father, or the father for his son,
We try to piece together the exploded fragments.
    Let these broken spars
Stand for the Armada and its proud full sails, for
    even if
The clock is put to rights, everyone will still
    believe it's fast:
The barman's shouts of *time* will be ignored in
    any case, since time
Is conversation; it is the hedge that flits
    incessantly into the present,
As words blossom from the speakers' mouths,
    and the flotilla returns to harbour,
Long after hours.

CIARAN CARSON

Poetical Epistle Tae Cullybackey Auld Nummer

Auld freen and helper up the hill,
By hamely words frae freedom's quill,
O' those wha doubly get their fill
      O' landlord laws,
True men shall thank you wae a will,
      An' help yer cause.

I watched you weel in years remote,
When bailiffs steered the tenants' boat,
How fearlessly you cast your vote
      On freedom's side;
Amang the first you tossed your coat
      'Gainst cursed pride.

You ne'er cud sympathize wae those
Wha havin' plucked at fortune's rose,
Wad straightway pawn their poorhouse clothes,
      And ape the Tory,
While ilka breath o' wind that blows
      Can sing their story.

sweaty

Can ony independent man,
Wha guides the plough wae wacket han',
While ill laws curse his native lan'
      In ilka way,
Bow down and serve the landlord clan
      For lickplate pay.

Still let us pride in takin' pert
Wae those wha thole oppression's dert,
Let's gae the twa-faced their dessert,
      And shut their mooth.
What though oor speech be sometimes tert,
      We'll tell the truth.

The tenants' war that round us rage,
Should a' oor noble thochts engage,
Until we wipe from freedom's page
        The ills that cover,
The homesteads o' the present age,
        And toss them over.

THOMAS GIVEN

Scribbled at a Cabinet Meeting

(Lloyd George speaks)

I curse the *optimistic* views of Haig – I don't
    believe'm
I curse the *pessimistic* views of Jellicoe – relieve
    him
Let Gough be sacked and Haig be damned
On justice let the door be slammed
Let gossip rule instead of law
I'll rule the services by jaw

SIR EDWARD CARSON

Vote for Lunn

For a man that's dedicated
with you at heart
vote for Lunn
and prove yourself smart!

ANON

'When Adam delf'

dug	When Adam delf
	and Eve span
ask if you want to prosper	spir if thou will spede
	whare was than
	the pride of man
mars/reward	that now merres his mede
	of erth and slame
as	als was Adam
afflictions	maked to noyes and nede
	ar we als he
	maked to be
	whil we this lif shall lede
	with I and E
	born ar we
promised	als Salomon us hight
	to travel here
alive	whils we are fere
	als fowls to the flight
	In world we ware
	cast for to care
until	to we be broght to wende
to happiness or woe	till wele or wa
one of those two	an of that twa
dwell	to won withouten ende
therefore	forthy whils thou
	may helpe thee now
	amend thee and haf minde
	when thou shall ga
will be your enemy	he bese thy fa
before	that ar was here thy frende
	with E and I
advise	I rede forthy

thou think upon thies thre
what we are
and what we ware
and what we shall be

War thou also wise

esteem   praised in price
also was Salomon

child   fairer fode
of bone and blode
then was Absalon
strengthy and strang

avenge   to wreke thy wrang
also ever was Sampson
thou ne might a day
na mare then thay

death   dede withstand alon
with I and E
dede to thee
shall com als I thee kenne

you don't know   thou ne wate
in what state
how ne whare ne when

ought   Of erth aght

that was bestowed on you   that thee was raght

promise   thou shall not have I hete

feet   bot seven fote

rot   therin to rote
and thy windingshete

therefore   forthy gif

while you're still alive   whils thou may lif

before all goes that you may get   or all gase that thou gete

your spirit from God   thy gast fra God

your goods dispersed   thy godes olod

trampled   thy flesh fouled under fete
with I and E

certain   siker thou be

executors	that they secutours
won't care	of thee ne will rek
guffaw and grab	bot skelk and skek
	full boldly in thy bowrs
	Of welth and wit
verified	this shall be hitt
	in world that thou here wroght
you must settle your account	reckon thou mon
give reasons	and yelde reson
for what you thought here	of thing that thou here thoght
sophism	may no falas
	help in this case
	ne counsel getes thou noght
no gift or favour	gift ne grace
works here	nane thare gase
but enjoy what you have bought	bot brok also thou hase boght
	with I and E
	the Boke biddes thee
	Man beware of thy werkes
time of the year	terme of the yere
	hase thou nan here
your reward is what you hit	thy mede bese ther thy merkes
	What may this be
	that I here se
beauty	the fairehede of thy face
colour	thy ble so bright
strength	thy main thy might
mouth that rejoices	thy mouth that miry mas
men	all mon als was
	to powder passe
look	to dede whan thou gase
guest	a grisely geste
	bese then thy breste
to	in armes til enbrase
	with I and E
secure	siker thou be

promise   thare es nane I thee hete
of all thy kith
wald slepe thee with
a night under shete

ANON

Boney

Oh Boney was a warrior
oh weigh heigh ya
a warrior and a terrior
John Browns war

Boney went acruising
oh weigh heigh ya
in the channel of old England
John Browns war

Nelson went also acruising
oh weigh heigh ya
he fought with noble Boney
John Browns war

He got sent to Saint Helena
oh weigh heigh ya
there he died a prisoner
John Browns war

ANON

The Glorious Strike of the Builders

They locked us out without a cause —
Our rights was our desires, —
We'll work for Trollope, Peto, Lucas,
For all the world, and Myers.

If we can only have our rights,
We will go to work much stronger —
Nine hours a day, that's what we say,
And not a moment longer.

ANON

from v.

'I've done my bits of mindless aggro too
not half a mile from where we're standing now.'
Yeah, ah bet yer wrote a poem, yer wanker you!
'No, shut yer gob a while. Ah'll tell yer 'ow . . .'

'Herman Darewski's band played operetta
with a wobbly soprano warbling. Just why
I made my mind up that I'd got to get her
with the fire hose I can't say, but I'll try.

It wasn't just the singing angered me.
At the same time half a crowd was jeering
as the smooth Hugh Gaitskell, our MP,
made promises the other half were cheering.

What I hated in those high soprano ranges
was uplift beyond all reason and control
and in a world where you say nothing changes
it seemed a sort of prick-tease of the soul.

I tell you when I heard high notes that rose
above Hugh Gaitskell's cool electioneering
straight from the warbling throat right up my
    nose
I had all your aggro in *my* jeering.

And I hit the fire extinguisher ON knob
and covered orchestra and audience with spray.
I could run as fast you then. A good job!
They yelled 'damned vandal' after me that
    day . . .'

And then yer saw the light and gave up 'eavy!
And knew a man's not how mu h he can sup . . .
Yer reward for growing up's this super-bevvy,
a meths and champagne punch in t'FA Cup.

Ah've 'eard all that from old farts past their
    prime.
'ow now yer live wi' all yer once detested . . .
Old farts with not much left'll give me time.
Fuckers like that get folk like me arrested.

Covet not thy neighbour's wife, thy neighbour's
    riches.
Vicar and cop who say, to save our souls,
Get thee beHind me, Satan, drop their breeches
and get the Devil's dick right up their 'oles!

It was more a *working* marriage that I'd meant,
a blend of masculine and feminine.
Ignoring me, he started looking, bent
on some more aerosolling, for his tin.

'It was more a *working* marriage that I mean!'
Fuck, and save mi soul, eh? That suits me.
Then as if I'd egged him on to be obscene
he added a middle slit to one daubed V.

Don't talk to me of fucking representing
the class yer were born into any more.
Yer going to get 'urt and start resenting
it's not poetry we need in this class war.

Yer've given yerself toffee, cunt. Who needs
yer fucking poufy words. Ah write mi own.
Ah've got mi work on show all ovver Leeds
like this UNITED 'ere on some sod's stone.

'OK!' (thinking I had him trapped) 'OK!'
'If you're so proud of it, then sign your name
when next you're full of HARP and armed with
    spray,
next time you take this short cut from the game.'

He took the can, contemptuous, unhurried
and cleared the nozzle and prepared to sign
the UNITED sprayed where mam and dad were
    buried.
He aerosolled his name. And it was mine.

The boy footballers bawl *Here Comes the Bride*
and drifting blossoms fall onto my head.
One half of me's alive but one half died
when the skin half sprayed my name among the
    dead.

Half versus half, the enemies within
the heart that can't be whole till they unite.
As I stoop to grab the crushed HARP lager tin
the day's already dusk, half dark, half light.

That UNITED that I'd wished onto the nation
or as reunion for dead parents soon recedes.
The word's once more a mindless desecration
by some HARPoholic yob supporting Leeds.

Almost the time for ghosts I'd better scram.
Though not given much to fears of spooky
    scaring
I don't fancy an encounter with mi mam
playing Hamlet with me for this swearing.

Though I've a train to catch my step is slow.
I walk on the grass and graves with wary tread
over these subsidences, these shifts below
the life of Leeds supported by the dead.

TONY HARRISON

A Lilliputian Ode on their Majesties' Accession

Smile, smile,
Blest isle!
Grief past,
At last,
Halcyon
Comes on.
New King,
Bells ring;
New Queen,
Blest scene!
Britain
Again
Revives
And thrives.
Fear flies,
Stocks rise;
Wealth flows,
Art grows.
Strange pack
Sent back;
Own folks

Crack jokes.
Those out
May pout;
Those in
Will grin.

Great, small,
Pleased all.

God send
No end
To line
Divine
Of George and Caroline!

HENRY CAREY

from The Bothie of Tober-Na-Vuolich

Somewhat more splendid in dress, in a waistcoat
    work of a lady,
Lindsay succeeded; the lively, the cheery, cigar-
    loving Lindsay,
Lindsay the ready of speech, the Piper, the
    Dialectician,
This was his title from Adam because of the
    words he invented,
Who in three weeks had created a dialect new for
    the party;
This was his title from Adam, but mostly they
    called him the Piper.
Lindsay succeeded, the lively, the cheery, cigar-
    loving Lindsay.
  Hewson and Hobbes were down at the
    matutine bathing; of course too
Arthur, the bather of bathers *par excellence*,
    Audley by surname,

Arthur they called him for love and for euphony;
    they had been bathing,
Where in the morning was custom, where over a
    ledge of granite
Into a granite basin the amber torrent descended,
Only a step from the cottage, the road and
    larches between them.
Hewson and Hobbes followed quick upon
    Adam; on them followed Arthur.
  Airlie descended the last, effulgent as god of
    Olympus;
Blue, perceptibly blue, was the coat that had
    white silk facings,
Waistcoat blue, coral-buttoned, the white-tie
    finely adjusted,
Coral moreover the studs on a shirt as of crochet
    of women:
When the fourwheel for ten minutes already had
    stood at the gateway,
He, like a god, came leaving his ample Olympian
    chamber.
  And in the fourwheel they drove to the place
    of the clansmen's meeting.
  So in the fourwheel they came; and Donald the
    innkeeper showed them
Up to the barn where the dinner should be. Four
    tables were in it;
Two at the top and the bottom, a little upraised
    from the level,
These for Chairman and Croupier, and gentry fit
    to be with them,
Two lengthways in the midst for keeper and gillie
    and peasant.
Here were clansmen many in kilt and bonnet
    assembled;
Keepers a dozen at least; the Marquis's targeted
    gillies;

Pipers five or six, among them the young one, the
    drunkard;
Many with silver brooches, and some with those
    brilliant crystals
Found amid granite-dust on the frosty scalp of
    the Cairn-Gorm;
But with snuff-boxes all, and all of them using
    the boxes.
Here too were Catholic Priest, and Established
    Minister standing;
Catholic Priest; for many still clung to the
    Ancient Worship,
And Sir Hector's father himself had built them a
    chapel;
So stood Priest and Minister, near to each other,
    but silent,
One to say grace before, the other after the
    dinner.
Hither anon too came the shrewd, ever-ciphering
    Factor,
Hither anon the Attaché, the Guardsman mute
    and stately,
Hither from lodge and bothie in all the adjoining
    shootings
Members of Parliament many, forgetful of votes
    and blue-books,
Here, amid heathery hills, upon beast and bird of
    the forest
Venting the murderous spleen of the endless
    Railway Committee.
Hither the Marquis of Ayr, and Dalgarnish Earl
    and Croupier,
And at their side, amid murmurs of welcome,
    long-looked for, himself too
Eager, the gray, but boy-hearted Sir Hector, the
    Chief and the Chairman.

ARTHUR HUGH CLOUGH

hut

Seasons

'I suppose the time will come'

I suppose the time will come
Aid it in the coming
When the Bird will crowd the Tree
And the Bee be booming.

I suppose the time will come
Hinder it a little
When the Corn in Silk will dress
And in Chintz the Apple

I believe the Day will be
When the Jay will giggle
At his new white House the Earth
That, too, halt a little –

EMILY DICKINSON

A Song for February

travelling

Day in an' day oot on his auld farrant loom,
    Time lengthens the wab o' the past;
Dame Nature steps in like a lamp tae the room,
Hir e'e tae the simmer o' life geein' bloom.
So winter slips by, wi' its mirth an' its gloom,
    As spring is appearin' at last.

The robin gets up an' he lauchs in his glee,
    In view o' the prospect so braw;

to one side

Sets his heid tae the side, wi' its feathers agee,
As he spies a bit snaw drop at fit o' the tree,

dainties/taste

An' says tae himsel' a'll hae denties tae pree
    By an' by when the splash is awa.

peeps/grass/hill

The blackbird keeks oot frae the fog at the broo,
   Gees his neb a bit dicht on a stane;
His eye caught the primrose appearin' in view,
An' the tiny wee violet o' Nature's ain blue;
He sung them a sang o' the auld an' the new –
   A sang we may a' let alane.

The thrush cuff't the leaves 'neath the skep o' the
                            bee,
   An' he tirrl't them aside wae a zest;
I maun hurry awa tae rehearsal, quo he,
This work fits the sparrow far better than me;
His sang pleased the ear frae the tap o' the tree
   As he fell intae tune wae the rest.

Thus Nature provides for hir hoose an' hir
kids   wanes,
   An' we may rejoice in the plan;
The wren tae the bluebonnet sings his refrain
paved area On causey o' cottier or lordly domain;
The wagtail looks on withoot shade o' disdain,
   May we aye say the same o' the man.

THOMAS GIVEN

The First Spring Day

I wonder if the sap is stirring yet,
If wintry birds are dreaming of a mate,
If frozen snowdrops feel as yet the sun
And crocus fires are kindling one by one:
   Sing, robin, sing;
I still am sore in doubt concerning Spring.

I wonder if the springtide of this year
Will bring another Spring both lost and dear;
If heart and spirit will find out their Spring,
Or if the world alone will bud and sing:
    Sing, hope, to me;
Sweet notes, my hope, soft notes for memory.

The sap will surely quicken soon or late,
The tardiest bird will twitter to a mate;
So Spring must dawn again with warmth and
   bloom,
Or in this world, or in the world to come:
    Sing, voice of Spring,
Till I too blossom and rejoice and sing.

CHRISTINA ROSSETTI

from Chansons Innocentes

in Just-
spring   when the world is mud-
luscious the little
lame balloonman

whistles   far   and wee

and eddieandbill come
running from marbles and
piracies and it's
spring

when the world is puddle-wonderful

the queer
old balloonman whistles
far   and   wee
and bettyandisbel come dancing

from hop-scotch and jump-rope and

it's
spring
and
   the

      goat-footed

balloonMan   whistles
far
and
wee

   e. e. cummings

What's in a Name?

Why has Spring one syllable less
Than any its fellow season?
There may be some other reason,
And I'm merely making a guess;
But surely it hoards such wealth
Of happiness, hope and health,
Sunshine and musical sound,
It may spare a foot from its name
Yet all the same
Superabound.

Soft-named Summer,
Most welcome comer,
Brings almost everything
Over which we dream or sing
Or sigh;
But then summer wends its way,
Tomorrow, – today, –
Good-bye!

Autumn, – the slow name lingers,
While we likewise flag;
It silences many singers;
Its slow days drag,
Yet hasten at speed
To leave us in chilly need
For Winter to strip indeed.

In all-lack Winter,
Dull of sense and of sound,
We huddle and shiver
Beside our splinter
Of crackling pine,
Snow in sky and snow on ground.
Winter and cold
Can't last for ever!
Today, tomorrow, the sun will shine;
When we are old,
But some still are young,
Singing the song
Which others have sung,
Ringing the bells
Which others have rung, –
Even so!
We ourselves, who else?
We ourselves long
Long ago.

CHRISTINA ROSSETTI

Fisherman's Rhyme

young A spraggy cod'll grow ni fatter
till it gits a sup o'new May watter

ANON

Summer Is By

(From the Irish)

Summer is by;
There is nae mair to tell.
Stark on the brae the stags bell:
snow The drift blaws oot o' the sky:
Summer is by.

waves Gulls frae the swaw lift owre
icy Wi' glaister'd wing;
tangled floor And cry through the switherin flurr
snowstorm O' the onding:

In their wrack the brackens lie
Black whaur they fell:
There is nae mair to tell:
Summer is by.

WILLIAM SOUTAR

Religion, Mystery

from John's Gospel

In the beginnin o aa things the Wurd wis there ense,
an the Wurd bade wi God, and the Wurd wis God.
He wis wi God i the beginnin, an aa things cam tae
be throu him, an wiout him no ae thing cam tae be.
Aathing at hes come tae be, he wis the life in it, an
that life wis the licht o man; an ey the licht shines i
the mirk, an the mirk downa slocken it nane.

There kythed a man, sent frae God, at his name
wis John. He cam for a witness, tae beir witness tae
the licht, at aa men micht win tae faith throu him.
He wisna the licht himsel; he cam tae beir witness
tae the licht. The true licht, at enlichtens ilka man,
wis een than comin intil the warld. He wis in the
warld, an the warld hed come tae be throu him, but
the warld miskent him. He cam tae the place at
belanged him, an them at belanged him walcomed-
him-na. But til aa sic as walcomed him he gae the
pouer tae become childer o God; een tae them at
pits faith in his name, an wis born, no o bluid or
carnal desire or the will o man, but o God.

Sae the Wurd becam flesh an made his wonnin
amang us, an we saw his glorie, sic glorie as belangs
the ae an ane Son o the Faither, fu o grace and
trowth. We hae John's witness til him: 'This is
him,' he cried out loud, 'at I spak o, whan I said,
"Him at is comin efter me is o heicher degree nor
me, because he wis there afore iver I wis born."'
Outo his fouth ilkane o us hes haen his skare, ay!
grace upò grace; for, athò the Law wis gíen throu
Moses, grace an trowth hes come throu Jesus
Christ. Nae man hes e'er seen God: but the ae an
ane Son, at is God himsel, an liggs on the briest o
the Faither, hes made him kent.

Trans. WILLIAM LAUGHTON LORIMER

already

cannot quench
appeared

dwelling

abundance

lies

'Levedy ic thonke thee'

lady Levedy ic thonke thee
very gentle wid herte swithe milde
for that good you have done me that god that thu havast idon me
  wid thine swete childe

  thu art god and swete and bright
from all others chosen of alle otheir icoren
creature of thee was that swete wight
  that was Jesus iboren

pray maide milde bidd I thee
  wid thine swete childe
shelter that thu herdie me
have/mercy to habben Godis milce

  moder loke one me
  wid thine swete eyen
  reste and blisse gef thu me
when my levedy then ic deyen

ANON

'I have a yong suster'

  I have a yong suster
  fer beyondyn the se
keepsakes many be the drowryis
  that che sente me

  che sente me the cherye
  withoutyn ony ston
dove and so che dede the dowe
  without ony bon

briar   sche sente me the brere
bark   withoutyn ony rynde
dear one   sche bad me love my lemman
                   withoute longgyng

                   how shuld ony cherye
                   be withoute ston?
                   and how shuld ony dowe
                   ben withoute bon?

                   how shuld ony brere
                   ben withoute rynde?
                   how shuld I love myn lemman
                   without longyng?

when   quan the cherye was a flour
                   than hadde it non ston
egg   quan the dowe was an ey
                   than hadde it non bon

in the seed   quan the brere was onbred
                   than hadde it non rynd
has what she loves quan the maydyn haght that che lovit
                   che is without longing

                        ANON

from Sir Gawain and the Green Knight

                        Mony klyf he overclambe in contrayes straunge
removed/as a stranger fer floten fro his frendes fremedly he rydes
bank/knight   at uche warthe other water ther the wyye passed
unusual   he fonde a foo hym byfore bot ferly hit were
had to   and that so foule and so felle that feght hym
                        byhode
among the hills so mony mervayl bi mount ther the mon fyndes
hard/part   hit were to tore for to telle of the tenthe dole

dragons	sumwhyle wyth wormes he werres and with wolves als
wild men/lived/crags	sumwhyle with wodwos that woned in the knarres
at other times	bothe wyth bulles and beres and bores otherquyle
giants/pursued	and etaynes that hym anelede of the heghe felle
if he hadn't/brave/enduring/God	nade he ben dughty and dryye and dryghtyn had served
killed	douteles he hade ben ded and dreped ful ofte
fighting/troubled	for werre wrathed hym not so much that wynter was wors
fell	when the colde cler water fro the cloudes schadde
froze/pale	and fres er hit falle myght on the fale erthe
armour	ner slayn wyth the slete he sleped in his yrnes
	mo nyghtes then innoghe in naked rokkes
stream	ther as claterande fro the crest the colde borne rennes
	and henged heghe over his hede in hard ysseikkles
	thus in peryle and payne and plytes ful harde
overland/rides	bi contray caryes this knyght tyl krystmasse even
alone	al one
	the knyght wel that tyde
complaint	to Mary made his mone
she/show/where	that ho hym red to ryde
guide/dwelling	and wysse hym to sum wone

ANON

A Charm Rhyme

This charme shall be said at night, or against night, about the place or feild, or about beasts without feild, and whosoever cometh in, he goeth not out for certaine.

On three crosses of a tree
three dead bodyes did hang
two were theeves
the third was Christ
on whom our beleife is
Dismas and Gesmas
Christ amidst them was
Dismas to heaven went
Gesmas to hell was sent
Christ that died on the roode
for Marie's love that by him stood
and through the vertue of his blood
Jesus save us and our good
within and without
and all this place about
and through the vertue of his might
lett noe theefe enter in this night
noe foote further in this place
that I upon goe
but at my bidding there be bound
to do all things that I bid them do
starke be their sinewes therewith
and their lives mightles
and their eyes sightles
dread and doubt
them enclose about
as a wall wrought of stone
so be the crampe in the ton
crampe and crookeing
and tault in their tooting
the might of the Trinity
save these goods and me

toes

in the name of Jesus holy benedicité
all about our goods bee
within and without
and all place about!

ANON

Hunting the Wren

We hunted the wren for Robin the Bobbin
we hunted the wren for Jack o'the Can
we hunted the wren for Robbin the Bobbin
we hunted the wren for ev'ry wan

ANON

from Dr Faustus

The clocke strikes eleaven.

Ah Faustus,
Now hast thou but one bare hower to live,
And then thou must be damnd perpetually:
Stand stil you ever mooving spheres of heaven,
That time may cease, and midnight never come:
Faire Natures eie, rise, rise againe, and make
Perpetuall day, or let this houre be but a yeere,
A moneth, a weeke, a naturall day,
That Faustus may repent, and save his soule,
O *lente lente currite noctis equi:*
The starres moove stil, time runs, the clocke wil
    strike,
The divel wil come, and Faustus must be damnd.
O Ile leape up to my God: who pulles me
    downe?
See see where Christs blood streames in the
    firmament,

One drop would save my soule, halfe a drop, ah
     my Christ,
Rend not my heart for naming of my Christ,
Yet wil I call on him, oh spare me Lucifer!
Where is it now? tis gone: and see where God
Stretcheth out his arme, and bends his irefull
     browes:
Mountaines and hilles, come, come and fall on me,
And hide me from the heavy wrath of God.
No no, then wil I headlong runne into the earth:
Earth gape, O no, it wil not harbour me:
You starres that raignd at my nativitie,
Whose influence hath alotted death and hel,
Now draw up Faustus like a foggy mist,
Into the intrailes of yon labring cloude,
That when you vomite foorth into the ayre,
My limbes may issue from your smoaky
     mouthes,
So that my soule may but ascend to heaven:
Ah, halfe the hower is past: *The watch strikes.*
Twil all be past anone:
Oh God, if thou wilt not have mercy on my
     soule,
Yet for Christs sake, whose bloud hath ransomd
     me,
Impose some end to my incessant paine,
Let Faustus live in hel a thousand yeeres,
A hundred thousand, and at last be sav'd.
O no end is limited to damned soules,
Why wert thou not a creature wanting soule?
Or, why is this immortall that thou hast?
Ah Pythagoras *metempsychosis* were that true,
This soule should flie from me, and I be changde
Unto some brutish beast:
Al beasts are happy, for when they die,
Their soules are soone dissolvd in elements,
But mine must live still to be plagde in hel:
Curst be the parents that ingendred me:

No Faustus, curse thy selfe, curse Lucifer,
That hath deprivde thee of the joyes of heaven:
                    The clocke striketh twelve.
O it strikes, it strikes, now body turne to ayre,
Or Lucifer wil beare thee quicke to hel:
                    Thunder and lightning.
Oh soule, be changde into little water drops,
And fal into the Ocean, nere be found:

My God, my God, looke not so fierce on me:
                              Enter divels.
Adders, and Serpents, let me breathe a while:
Ugly hell gape not, come not Lucifer,
Ile burne my bookes, ah Mephastophilis.
                              Exeunt with him.

CHRISTOPHER MARLOWE

'This is my playes last scene'

This is my playes last scene, here heavens appoint
My pilgrimages last mile; and my race
Idly, yet quickly runne, hath this last pace,
My spans last inch, my minutes latest point,
And gluttonous death, will instantly unjoynt
My body, and my soule, and I shall sleepe a
    space,
But my ever-waking part shall see that face,
Whose feare already shakes my every joynt:
Then, as my soule, to heaven her first seate, takes
    flight,
And earth borne body, in the earth shall dwell,
So, fall my sinnes, that all may have their right,

To where they are bred, and would presse me, to
   hell.
Impute me righteous, thus purg'd of evill,
For thus I leave the world, the flesh the devill.

    JOHN DONNE

'If poysonous mineralls'

If poysonous mineralls, and if that tree,
Whose fruit threw death on else immortall us,
If lecherous goats, if serpents envious
Cannot be damn'd; Alas; why should I bee?
Why should intent or reason, borne in mee,
Make sinnes, else equall, in mee, more heinous?
And mercy being easie, and glorious
To God, in his sterne wrath, why threatens hee?
But who am I, that dare dispute with thee?
O God, Oh! of thine onely worthy blood,
And my teares, make a heavenly Lethean flood,
And drowne in it my sinnes blacke memorie,
That thou remember them, some claime as debt,
I thinke it mercy, if thou wilt forget.

    JOHN DONNE

The Collar

    I struck the board, and cry'd, No more.
        I will abroad.
   What? shall I ever sigh and pine?
My lines and life are free; free as the rode,
   Loose as the winde, as large as store.
      Shall I be still in suit?

Have I no harvest but a thorn
To let me bloud, and not restore
What I have lost with cordiall fruit?
                    Sure there was wine
        Before my sighs did drie it: there was corn
                Before my tears did drown it.
        Is the yeare onely lost to me?
                Have I no bayes to crown it?
No flowers, no garlands gay? all blasted?
            All wasted?
        No so, my heart: but there is fruit,
                And thou hast hands.
            Recover all thy sigh-blown age
On double pleasures: leave thy cold dispute
Of what is fit, and not. Forsake thy cage,
                Thy rope of sands,
Which pettie thoughts have made, and made to
                                    thee
        Good cable, to enforce and draw,
                And be thy law,
        While thou didst wink and wouldst not see.
                Away; take heed:
                I will abroad.
Call in thy deaths head there: tie up thy fears.
                He that forbears
            To suit and serve his need,
                Deserves his load.
But as I rav'd and grew more fierce and wilde
            At every word,
Me thoughts I heard one calling, *Child*:
            And I reply'd, *My Lord*.

GEORGE HERBERT

The Answer

My comforts drop and melt away like snow:
I shake my head, and all the thoughts and ends,
Which my fierce youth did bandie, fall and flow
Like leaves about me: or like summer friends,
Flyes of estates and sunne-shine. But to all,
Who think me eager, hot, and undertaking,
But in my prosecutions slack and small;
As a young exhalation, newly waking,
Scorns his first bed of dirt, and means the sky;
But cooling by the way, grows pursie and slow,
And setling to a cloud, doth live and die
In that dark state of tears: to all, that so
     Show me, and set me, I have one reply,
      Which they that know the rest, know more
                      than I.

GEORGE HERBERT

Love

Love bade me welcome: yet my soul drew
                    back,
     Guiltie of dust and sinne.
But quick-ey'd Love, observing me grow slack
     From my first entrance in,
Drew nearer to me, sweetly questioning,
     If I lack'd any thing.

A guest, I answer'd, worthy to be here:
     Love said, You shall be he.
I the unkinde, ungratefull? Ah my deare,
     I cannot look on thee.
Love took my hand, and smiling did reply,
     Who made the eyes but I?

Truth Lord, but I have marr'd them: let my
shame
Go where it doth deserve.
And know you not, sayes Love, who bore the
blame?
My deare, then I will serve.
You must sit down, sayes Love, and taste my
meat:
So I did sit and eat.

GEORGE HERBERT

Employment

He that is weary, let him sit.
My soul would stirre
And trade in courtesies and wit,
Quitting the furre
To cold complexions needing it.

Man is no starre, but a quick coal
Of mortall fire:
Who blows it not, nor doth controll
A faint desire,
Lets his own ashes choke his soul.

When th' elements did for place contest
With him, whose will
Ordain'd the highest to be best;
The earth sat still,
And by the others is opprest.

Life is a businesse, not good cheer;
Ever in warres.
The sunne still shineth there or here,
Whereas the starres
Watch an advantage to appeare.

Oh that I were an Orenge-tree,
                That busie plant!
Then should I ever laden be,
                And never want
Some fruit for him that dressed me.

But we are still too young or old;
                The man is gone,
Before we do our wares unfold:
                So we freeze on,
Untill the grave increase our cold.

GEORGE HERBERT

Tayis Bank

Quhen Tayis bank wes blumyt brycht
broad   with blosomes blyth and bred
be that rever ran I doun rycht
bough / rode   undir the rys I red
blackbird / mingled (notes)   the merle melit with all hir mycht
and mirth in mornyng maid
throw solace sound and semely sicht
at once   alsuth a sang I said

Undir that bank quhair blis had bene
prepared myself   I bownit me to abide
holly tree   ane holene hevinly hewit grene
graciously   rycht heyndly did me hyd
woods / beautiful   the sone schyne our the schawis schene
full semely me besyd
arrayed   in bed of blumes bricht besene
did   a sleip couth me ourslyd

About all blomet wes my bour
with blosummes broun and blew
adorned   ourfret with mony fair fresch flour
wholesome helsum of hevinly hew
quivering   with schakeris of the schene dew schour
curtains   schynnyng my courtenis schew
verdure   arrayit with a rich vardour
of natouris werkis new

Rasing the birdis fra thair rest
beams   the reid sone rais with rawis
the lark sang loud quhill lycht mycht lest
a lay of luvis lawis
the nythingall woik of hir nest
dawns   singing *The day updawis*
the mirthfull maveis merriest
shrill   schill schowttit throw the schawis

grove   All flouris grew that firth within
could   that man couth haif in mind,
and in that flud all fische with fin
that creat wer be kind
roe   undir the rise the ra did ryn
small stream/bark our ron our rute our rind
the dun deir dansit with a din
and herdis of hairt and hind

mad/wallowing Wod Winter with his wallowand wind
doubt   but weir away wes went
embraced   brasit about with wild wodbynd
open ground wer bewis on the bent
allone under the lusty lind
lovesome one lingering I saw ane lusum lent
wonderful   that fairly war so fare to find
undir the firmament

Scho wes the lustiest on live

on land   allone lent on a land

by far   and farest figour be sic syve

that evir in firth I fand

describe   hir cumly cullour to discryve

undertake   I dar nocht tak on hand

moir womanly borne of a wife

wes never I dar warrand

To creatur that wes in cair

or cauld of crewelty

blythe glance   a blicht blenk of hir vesage bair

help   of baill his bute mycht be

hir hyd hir hew hir hevinly hair

uplift   mycht havy hairtis uphie

so angelik under the air

never wicht I saw with e

The blosummes that wer blyth and bricht

bleached   by hir wer blacht and blew

scho gladit all the foull of flicht

that in the forrest flew

scho mycht haif comfort king or knycht

that ever in cuntre I knew

choice   as waill and well of warldly wicht

in womanly vertew

Hir cullour cleir hir countinance

hir cumly cristall ene

figure   hir portratour of most plesance

surpass   all pictour did prevene

commend   off every vertew to avance

quhen ladeis prasit bene

rychttest in my remmembrance

that rose is rutit grene

gentle   This mild meik mansuet Margrite
                     this perle polist most quhyt
                     dame natouris deir dochter discreit
                     the dyamant of delyt
travel on foot   never formit wes to found on feit
                     ane figour moir perfyte
on earth   nor non on mold that did hir meit
improve/in any way   mycht mend hir wirth a mite

tried   This mirthful maid to meit I ment
moved forward   and merkit furth on mold
dwelling   but sone within a wane scho went
                     most hevinly to behold
glanced   the bricht sone with his bemys blent
breastworks   upoun the bertis bold
                     farest under the firmament
on earth   that formit wes on fold

                     As parradice that place but peir
                     wes plesand to my sicht
                     of forrest and of fresch reveir
                     of firth and fowll of flicht
song/bank/briar   of birdis bay on bonk and breir
                     with blumes brekand bricht
                     as hevin in to this erd doun heir
on high   hertis to hald on hicht

                     So went this womanly away
                     amang thir woddis wyd
                     and I to heir thir birdis gay
                     did in a bonk abyd
                     quhair ron and rys rais in aray
                     endlang the rever syd
                     this hapnit me in a time in May
                     in till a morning tyd

roar   The rever throw the rise couth rowt
rosebushes/rose/in a row   and roseris rais on raw.
                          the schene birdis full schill couth schowt
                          into that semly schaw
                          joy wes within and joy without
fairest wall   under that wlonkest waw
                          quhair Tay ran doun with stremis stout
                          full strecht under Stobschaw

                               ANON

Christmas Rhyme: North Tyrone

First Player: What is your plaster Doctor?
Doctor: Hens pens peesy weesy midges eyes bum bees
                        bacon
                   the juice of the riddle the sap of the tongs
                   three duck eggs nine yards long
                   all put in a bladder and stirred with a grey cats
                        feather
                   put in a jolly mans stockings as tight as he can
endure   thole
                   three weeks before the sun rises and a fortnight
                        after she sets
                   to spit as straight as a rush in the neck of a
                        tuppenny bottle
                   if that does not cure him the devil may cure
                        him
                   for I'll not cure him tonight sir

Beelzebub: Here comes I Beelzebub
and over my shoulder I carry my club
in my hand a dripping pan
I think myself a jolly old man
last Christmas night I turned the spit
I burnt my finger and feel it yet
between my finger and my thumb
there rose a blister as big as a plum
and it's not away yet
I took out my pipe and began to smoke
until the slavers ran down the back of my coat
up jumps the cock sparrow and flew across the
    table
up jumps the wee pot and began to play with the
    ladle
up jumps the dishcloth and all its dirty duds
and up jumps the besom between the two lugs
up jumps the beetle saying can you not agree
send for Mick Murphy and bring him here to me
when Mick Murphy came there he had a belly as
    big as a bear
he ate a cow he ate a bullock and a half
he licked the ladle swallowed the spoon
and wasn't foo when all was done
if you don't believe me what I say
enter in Oliver Cromwell and he will clear the
    way

ANON

from The Wreck of the Deutschland

Sister, a sister calling
A master, her master and mine! –
And the inboard seas run swirling and hawling;
The rash smart sloggering brine
Blinds her; but she that weather sees one thing, one;
Has one fetch in her: she rears herself to divine
Ears, and the call of the tall nun
To the men in the tops and the tackle rode over the storm's brawling.

She was first of a five and came
Of a coifèd sisterhood.
(O Deutschland, double a desperate name!
O world wide of its good!
But Gertrude, lily, and Luther, are two of a town,
Christ's lily and beast of the waste wood:
From life's dawn it is drawn down,
Abel is Cain's brother and breasts they have sucked the same.)

Loathed for a love men knew in them,
Banned by the land of their birth,
Rhine refused them, Thames would ruin them;
Surf, snow, river and earth
Gnashed: but thou art above, thou Orion of light;
Thy unchancelling poising palms were weighing the worth,
Thou martyr-master: in thy sight
Storm flakes were scroll-leaved flowers, lily showers – sweet heaven
    was astrew in them.

Five! the finding and sake
And cipher of suffering Christ.
Mark, the mark is of man's make
And the word of it Sacrificed.
But he scores it in scarlet himself on his own bespoken,
Before-time-taken, dearest prizèd and priced –
Stigma, signal, cinquefoil token
For lettering of the lamb's fleece, ruddying of the rose-flake.

Joy fall to thee, father Francis,
Drawn to the Life that died;
With the gnarls of the nails in thee, niche of the lance, his
Lovescape crucified
And seal of his seraph-arrival! and these thy daughters
And five-livèd and leavèd favour and pride,
Are sisterly sealed in wild waters,
To bathe in his fall-gold mercies, to breathe in his all-fire glances.

Away in the lovable west,
On a pastoral forehead of Wales,
I was under a roof here, I was at rest,
And they the prey of the gales;
She to the black-about air, to the breaker, the thickly
Falling flakes, to the throng that catches and quails
Was calling 'O Christ, Christ, come quickly':
The cross to her she calls Christ to her, christens her wild-worst Best.

The majesty! what did she mean?
Breathe, arch and original Breath.
Is it love in her of the being as her lover had been?
Breathe, body of lovely Death.
They were else-minded then, altogether, the men
Woke thee with a *We are perishing* in the weather of Gennesareth.
Or is it that she cried for the crown then,
The keener to come at the comfort for feeling the combating keen?

For how to the heart's cheering
The down-dugged ground-hugged grey
Hovers off, the jay-blue heavens appearing
Of pied and peeled May!
Blue-beating and hoary-glow height; or night, still higher,
With belled fire and the moth-soft Milky Way,
What by your measure is the heaven of desire,
The treasure never eyesight got, nor was ever guessed what for the
hearing?

No, but it was not these.
The jading and jar of the cart,
Time's tasking, it is fathers that asking for ease
Of the sodden-with-its-sorrowing heart,
Not danger, electrical horror; then further it finds
The appealing of the Passion is tenderer in prayer apart:
Other, I gather, in measure her mind's
Burden, in wind's burly and beat of endragonèd seas.

But how shall I . . . make me room there:
Reach me a . . . Fancy, come faster —
Strike you the sight of it? look at it loom there,
Thing that she . . . There then! the Master,
Ipse, the only one, Christ, King, Head:
He was to cure the extremity where he had cast her;
Do, deal, lord it with living and dead;
Let him ride, her pride, in his triumph, despatch and have done with
his doom there.

Ah! there was a heart right!
There was single eye!
Read the unshapeable shock night
And knew the who and the why;
Wording it how but by him that present and past,
Heaven and earth are word of, worded by? —
The Simon Peter of a soul! to the blast
Tarpeïan-fast, but a blown beacon of light.

Jesu, heart's light,
Jesu, maid's son,
What was the feast followed the night
Thou hadst glory of this nun? —
Feast of the one woman without stain.
For so conceivèd, so to conceive thee is done;
But here was heart-throe, birth of a brain,
Word, that heard and kept thee and uttered thee outright.

Well, she has thee for the pain, for the
Patience; but pity of the rest of them!
Heart, go and bleed at a bitterer vein for the
Comfortless unconfessed of them –
No not uncomforted: lovely-felicitous Providence
Finger of a tender of, O of a feathery delicacy, the breast of the
Maiden could obey so, be a bell to, ring of it, and
Startle the poor sheep back! is the shipwrack then a harvest, does
tempest carry the grain for thee?

I admire thee, master of tides,
Of the Yore-flood, of the year's fall;
The recurb and the recovery of the gulf's sides,
The girth of it and the wharf of it and the wall;
Stanching, quenching ocean of a motionable mind;
Ground of being, and granite of it: past all
Grasp God, throned behind
Death with a sovereignty that heeds but hides, bodes but abides;

With a mercy that outrides
The all of water, an ark
For the listener; for the lingerer with a love glides
Lower than death and the dark;
A vein for the visiting of the past-prayer, pent in prison,
The-last-breath penitent spirits – the uttermost mark
Our passion-plungèd giant risen,
The Christ of the Father compassionate, fetched in the storm of his
strides.

Now burn, new born to the world,
Double-naturèd name,
The heaven-flung, heart-fleshed, maiden-furled
Miracle-in-Mary-of-flame,
Mid-numberèd he in three of the thunder-throne!
Not a dooms-day dazzle in his coming nor dark as he came;
Kind, but royally reclaiming his own;
A released shower, let flash to the shire, not a lightning of fire hard-
hurled.

Dame, at our door
Drowned, and among our shoals,
Remember us in the roads, the heaven-haven of the reward:
Our King back, Oh, upon English souls!
Let him easter in us, be a dayspring to the dimness of us, be a
crimson-cresseted east,
More brightening her, rare-dear Britain, as his reign rolls,
Pride, rose, prince, hero of us, high-priest,
Our hearts' charity's hearth's fire, our thoughts' chivalry's throng's
Lord.

GERARD MANLEY HOPKINS

Felix Randal

Felix Randal the farrier, O is he dead? my duty
    all ended,
Who have watched his mould of man, big-boned
    and hardy-handsome
Pining, pining, till time when reason rambled in it
    and some
Fatal four disorders, fleshed there, all contended?

Sickness broke him. Impatient, he cursed at first,
    but mended
Being anointed and all; though a heavenlier heart
    began some
Holy Communion   Months earlier, since I had our sweet reprieve
    and ransom
in whatever way   Tendered to him. Ah well, God rest him all road
    ever he offended!

This seeing the sick endears them to us, us too it
    endears.
My tongue had taught thee comfort, touch had
    quenched thy tears,
Thy tears that touched my heart, child, Felix,
    poor Felix Randal;

How far from then forethought of, all thy more
    boisterous years,
When thou at the random grim forge, powerful
    amidst peers,
prepare   Didst fettle for the great grey drayhorse his bright
    and battering sandal!

GERARD MANLEY HOPKINS

'I wake and feel the fell of dark, not day'

I wake and feel the fell of dark, not day.
What hours, O what black hoürs we have spent
This night! what sights you, heart, saw; ways you
    went!
And more must, in yet longer light's delay.

With witness I speak this. But where I say
Hours I mean years, mean life. And my lament
Is cries countless, cries like dead letters sent
To dearest him that lives alas! away.

I am gall, I am heartburn. God's most deep
    decree
Bitter would have me taste: my taste was me;
Bones built in me, flesh filled, blood brimmed the
    curse.

Selfyeast of spirit a dull dough sours. I see
The lost are like this, and their scourge to be
As I am mine, their sweating selves; but worse.

GERARD MANLEY HOPKINS

That Nature is a Heraclitean Fire and of the comfort of the Resurrection

Cloud-puffball, torn tufts, tossed pillows ˡ flaunt
scamper   forth, then chevy on an air-
built thoroughfare; heaven-roysterers, in gay-
      gangs ˡ they throng; they glitter in marches.
Down roughcast, down dazzling whitewash, ˡ
      wherever an elm arches,
strips of light Shivelights and shadowtackle in long ˡ lashes
      lace, lance, and pair.
Delightfully the bright wind boisterous ˡ ropes,
      wrestles, beats earth bare
Of yestertempest's creases; ˡ in pool and rutpeel
      parches
Squandering ooze to squeezed ˡ dough, crust,
      dust; staunches, starches
Squadroned masks and manmarks ˡ treadmire toil
      there
Footfretted in it. Million-fuelèd, ˡ nature's bonfire
      burns on.
But quench her bonniest, dearest ˡ to her, her
      clearest-selvèd spark
Man, how fast his firedint, ˡ his mark on mind, is
      gone!
Both are in an unfathomable, all is in an
      enormous dark
Drowned. O pity and indig ˡ nation! Manshape,
      that shone
separate and aloof Sheer off, disseveral, a star, ˡ death blots black
      out; nor mark
                      Is any of him at all so stark
But vastness blurs and time ˡ beats level. Enough!
      the Resurrection,

A heart's-clarion! Away grief's gasping, | joyless
   days, dejection.
                       Across my foundering deck
   shone
A beacon, an eternal beam. | Flesh fade, and
   mortal trash
Fall to the residuary worm; | world's wildfire,
   leave but ash:
                   In a flash, at a trumpet crash,
I am all at once what Christ is, | since he was
   what I am, and
fool   This Jack, joke, poor potsherd, | patch,
   matchwood, immortal diamond,
                  Is immortal diamond.

GERARD MANLEY HOPKINS

from The Author's Apology for his Book

When at the first I took my Pen in hand,
Thus for to write; I did not understand
That I at all should make a little Book
In such a mode; Nay, I had undertook
To make another, which when almost done,
Before I was aware, I this begun.
   And thus it was: I writing of the Way
And Race of Saints in this our Gospel-Day,
Fell suddenly into an Allegory
About their Journey, and the way to Glory,
In more than twenty things, which I set down;
This done, I twenty more had in my Crown,
And they again began to multiply,
Like sparks that from the coals of Fire do flie.
Nay then, thought I, if that you breed so fast,
I'll put you by your selves, lest you at last
Should prove *ad infinitum*, and eat out
The Book that I already am about.

Well, so I did; but yet I did not think
To shew to all the World my Pen and Ink
In such a mode; I only thought to make
I knew not what: nor did I undertake
Thereby to please my Neighbour; no not I,
I did it mine own self to gratifie.

Neither did I but vacant seasons spend
In this my Scribble; Nor did I intend
But to divert my self in doing this,
From worser thoughts, which make me do amiss.

Thus I set Pen to Paper with delight,
And quickly had my thoughts in black and white.
For having now my Method by the end;
Still as I pull'd, it came; and so I penn'd
It down, until it came at last to be
For length and breadth the bigness which you see.

Well, when I had thus put mine ends together,
I shew'd them others, that I might see whether
They would condemn them, or them justifie:
And some said, let them live; some, let them die:
Some said, *John*, print it; others said, Not so:
Some said, It might do good; others said, No.

Now was I in a straight, and did not see
Which was the best thing to be done by me:
At last I thought, Since you are thus divided,
I print it will, and so the case decided.

For, thought I; Some I see would have it done,
Though others in that Channel do not run;
To prove then who advised for the best,
Thus I thought fit to put it to the test.

I further thought, if now I did deny
Those that would have it thus, to gratifie,
I did not know, but hinder them I might,
Of that which would to them be great delight.

For those that were not for its coming forth;
I said to them, Offend you I am loth;
Yet since your Brethren pleased with it be,
Forbear to judge, till you do further see.

If that thou wilt not read, let it alone;
Some love the meat, some love to pick the bone:
Yea, that I might them better palliate,
I did too with them thus Expostulate.

   May I not write in such a stile as this?
In such a method too, and yet not miss
Mine end, thy good? why may it not be done?
Dark Clouds bring Waters, when the bright bring
                                        none;
Yea, dark, or bright, if they their silver drops
Cause to descend, the Earth, by yielding Crops,
Gives praise to both, and carpeth not at either,
But treasures up the Fruit they yield together:
Yea, so commixes both, that in her Fruit
None can distinguish this from that, they suit
Her well, when hungry: but if she be full,
She spues out both, and makes their blessings
                                        null.

   You see the ways the Fisher-man doth take
To catch the Fish; what Engins doth he make?
Behold! how he ingageth all his Wits;
Also his Snares, Lines, Angles, Hooks and Nets;
Yet Fish there be, that neither Hook, nor Line,
Nor Snare, nor Net, nor Engin can make thine;
They must be grop'd for, and be tickled too,
Or they will not be catcht, what e'er you do.

   How doth the Fowler seek to catch his Game,
By divers means, all which one cannot name?
His Gun, his Nets, is Lime-twigs, light and bell:
He creeps, he goes, he stands; yea, who can tell
Of all his postures? Yet there's none of these
Will make him master of what Fowls he please.
Yea, he must Pipe, and Whistle to catch *this*;
Yet if he does so, *that* Bird he will miss.

   If that a Pearl may in a Toads-head dwell,
And may be found too in an Oister-shell;
If things that promise nothing, do contain
What better is then Gold; who will disdain,

(That have an inkling of it,) there to look,
That they may find it? Now my little Book,
(Tho void of all those paintings that may make
It with this or the other man to take,)
Is not without those things that do excel,
What do in brave, but empty notions dwell.

Well, yet I am not fully satisfied,
That this your Book will stand, when soundly
                                        try'd.

Why, what's the matter? *It is dark*, what tho?
But it is feigned, what of that I tro?
Some men by feigning words as dark as mine,
Make truth to spangle, and its rayes to shine.

But they want solidness: Speak man thy mind:
They drown'd the weak; Metaphors make us
                                        blind.

Solidity, indeed becomes the Pen
Of him that writeth things Divine to men:
But must I needs want solidness, because
By Metaphors I speak; was not Gods Laws,
His Gospel-laws in olden time held forth
By Types, Shadows and Metaphors? Yet loth
Will any sober man be to find fault
With them, lest he be found for to assault
The highest Wisdom. No, he rather stoops,
And seeks to find out what by pins and loops,
By Calves, and Sheep; by Heifers, and by Rams;
By Birds and Herbs, and by the blood of Lambs;
God speaketh to him: And happy is he
That finds the light, and grace that in them be.

JOHN BUNYAN

from Jubilate Agno

Rejoice in God, O ye Tongues; give the glory to
the Lord, and the Lamb.

Nations, and languages, and every Creature, in
which is the breath of Life.

Let man and beast appear before him, and
magnify his name together.

Let Noah and his company approach the throne
of Grace, and do homage to the Ark of their
Salvation.

Let Abraham present a Ram, and worship the
God of his Redemption.

Let Isaac, the Bridegroom, kneel with his Camels,
and bless the hope of his pilgrimage.

Let Jacob, and his speckled Drove adore the good
Shepherd of Israel.

Let Esau offer a scape Goat for his seed, and
rejoice in the blessing of God his father.

Let Nimrod, the mighty hunter, bind a Leopard
to the altar, and consecrate his spear to the
Lord.

Let Ishmael dedicate a Tyger, and give praise for
the liberty, in which the Lord has let him at
large.

Let Balaam appear with an Ass, and bless the
Lord his people and his creatures for a reward
eternal.

Let Anah, the son of Zibion, lead a Mule to the
temple, and bless God, who amerces the
consolation of the creature for the service of
Man.

Let Daniel come forth with a Lion, and praise
God with all his might through faith in Christ
Jesus.

Let Naphthali with an Hind give glory in the
goodly words of Thanksgiving.

Let Aaron, the high priest, sanctify a Bull, and let
  him go free to the Lord and Giver of Life.
Let the Levites of the Lord take the Beavers of
  the brook alive into the Ark of the Testimony.
Let Eleazar with the Ermine serve the Lord
  decently and in purity.
Let Ithamar minister with a Chamois, and bless
  the name of Him, which cloatheth the naked.

hart

Let Gershom with an Pygarg bless the name of
  Him, who feedeth the hungry.
Let Merari praise the wisdom and power of God
  with the Coney, who scoopeth the rock, and
  archeth in the sand.
Let Kohath serve with the Sable, and bless God
  in the ornaments of the Temple.
Let Jehoida bless God with an Hare, whose
  mazes are determined for the health of the
  body and to parry the adversary.

*

Let Anaiah bless with the Dragon-fly, who sails
  over the pond by the wood-side and feedeth on
  the cressies.
Let Zorobabel bless with the Wasp, who is the
  Lord's architect, and buildeth his edifice in
  armour.
Let Jehu bless with the Hornet, who is the soldier
  of the Lord to extirpate abomination and to
  prepare the way of peace.
Let Mattithiah bless with the Bat, who inhabiteth
  the desolations of pride and flieth amongst the
  tombs.
Let Elias which is the innocency of the Lord
  rejoice with the Dove.
Let Asaph rejoice with the Nightingale – The
  musician of the Lord! and the watchman of the
  Lord!

Let Shema rejoice with the Glowworm, who is
   the lamp of the traveller and mead of the
   musician.
Let Jeduthun rejoice with the Woodlark, who is
   sweet and various.
Let Chenaniah rejoice with Chloris, in the
   vivacity of his powers and the beauty of his
   person.
Let Gideoni rejoice with the Goldfinch, who is
   shrill and loud, and full withal.
Let Giddalti rejoice with the Mocking-bird, who
   takes off the notes of the Aviary and reserves
   his own.
Let Jogli rejoice with the Linnet, who is distinct
   and of mild delight.
Let Benjamin bless and rejoice with the Redbird,
   who is soft and soothing.
Let Dan rejoice with the Blackbird, who praises
   God with all his heart, and biddeth to be of
   good cheer.

CHRISTOPHER SMART

'Oh trial'

Oh trial!
great trevelation children ho!
trial!
we bound t'leave dis world
Baptis Baptis
Baptis till I die
I been grown up in the Baptis side
an die under Baptis rule
oh trial!
great trevelation children ho!
trial!
we bound t'leave dis world

church light   church light
church light till I die
I been grown up in the church light side
an die under church light rule
oh trial!
great trevelation children ho!
trial!
we bound t'leave dis world

ANON

The Twins

'Give' and 'It-shall-be-given-unto-you'.

I

Grand rough old Martin Luther
   Bloomed fables – flowers on furze,
The better the uncouther:
   Do roses stick like burrs?

II

A beggar asked an alms
   One day at an abbey-door,
Said Luther; but, seized with qualms,
   The Abbot replied, 'We're poor!

III

'Poor, who had plenty once,
   'When gifts fell thick as rain:
'But they give us nought, for the nonce,
   'And how should we give again?'

IV

Then the beggar, 'See your sins!
   'Of old, unless I err,
'Ye had brothers for inmates, twins,
   'Date and Dabitur.

IV

'While Date was in good case
 'Dabitur flourished too:
'For Dabitur's lenten face
 'No wonder if Date rue.

VI

'Would ye retrieve the one?
 'Try and make plump the other!
'When Date's penance is done,
 'Dabitur helps his brother.

VII

'Only, beware relapse!'
 The Abbot hung his head.
This beggar might be perhaps
 An angel, Luther said.

ROBERT BROWNING

from Mark's Gospel

Aa this while, Peter wis doun ablò i the yaird. As he

warming

wis sittin there beikin himsel at the fire, ane o the
Heid-Príest's servan-queans cam in an, seein him,
tuik a guid luik o him an said, 'Ye war wi the man
frae Nazareth, this Jesus, tae, I'm thinkin.'

nothing at all

But he wadna own wi it: 'I kenna buff nor sty
what ye're speakin o,' said he; an wi that he slippit

porch

out intil the fore-close.

The servan-lass saw him there an said tae the

lad

staunders-by, 'This chíel's ane o them': but aince
mair he denied it.

soon

Belyve the staunders-by cam back til it an said
tae Peter: 'Deed, but ye ar sae ane o them; ye'r frae
Galilee!'

cursing

   At that he set tae the bannin an swuir at he kentna 'this man,' says he, 'at ye'r speakin o.' Nae shuner wis the wurds out o his mou nor the cock crew the saicond time. Than Peter caa'd tae mind hou Jesus hed sayen til him, 'Afore the cock craw twice, ye will disavou me thrice.' An he banged out an fell agreitin.

rushed

began weeping

Trans. WILLIAM LAUGHTON LORIMER

In the Servants' Quarters

'Man, you too, aren't you, one of these rough
    followers of the criminal?
All hanging hereabout to gather how he's going
    to bear
Examination in the hall.' She flung disdainful
    glances on
The shabby figure standing at the fire with others
    there,
        Who warmed them by its flare.

'No indeed, my skipping maiden: I know nothing
    of the trial here,
Or criminal, if so he be. – I chanced to come this
    way,
And the fire shone out into the dawn, and
    morning airs are cold now;
I, too, was drawn in part by charms I see before
    me play,
        That I see not every day.'

'Ha, ha!' then laughed the constables who also
 stood to warm themselves,
The while another maiden scrutinized his features
 hard,
As the blaze threw into contrast every line and
 knot that wrinkled them,
Exclaiming, 'Why, last night when he was
 brought in by the guard,
   You were with him in the yard!'

'Nay, nay, you teasing wench, I say! You know
 you speak mistakenly.
Cannot a tired pedestrian who has legged it long
 and far
Here on his way from northern parts, engrossed
 in humble marketings,
Come in and rest a while, although judicial
 doings are
   Afoot by morning star?'

'O, come, come!' laughed the constables. 'Why,
 man, you speak the dialect
He uses in his answers; you can hear him up the
 stairs.
So own it. We sha'n't hurt ye. There he's
 speaking now! His syllables
Are those you sound yourself when you are
 talking unawares,
   As this pretty girl declares.'

'And you shudder when his chain clinks!' she
   rejoined. 'O yes, I noticed it.
And you winced, too, when those cuffs they gave
   him echoed to us here.
They'll soon be coming down, and you may then
   have to defend yourself
Unless you hold your tongue, or go away and
   keep you clear
       When he's led to judgment near!'

'No! I'll be damned in hell if I know anything
   about the man!
No single thing about him more than everybody
   knows!
Must not I even warm my hands but I am
   charged with blasphemies?' . . .
— His face convulses as the morning cock that
   moment crows,
       And he droops, and turns, and goes.

THOMAS HARDY

from Memres of Alfred Stoker

firs
born X mas day
Yer 1885
in the same burer Waping

pa a way
Ma not
being by Trade merchent Sea man
in forn parts:
all so a precher
on Land

i sow him Latter

4 of 9
not all Livig

a hard Thing Ma sad:
mirs Pale a mid Wife
in the back room bed rom
Nor wod she got Thurgh
when a ANGEL apperd over the JESUS pichire
which i got after
it Savd my Life.

                                        *

so i name Gabriel
which you did not no why shod you
onlie its Secd
Alfred Gabriel Joseph Stoker
Like that.

some recked she was Ling
but she was not
the ANGEL was Trew.

He had a Gold face she sad:
and his Winges Gold flammy
and his ramond of Gold stufes

and in his hand he bare a BIBLE of Gold paper
and his Vois was as the Claper of Thunder over
    hede
with Gold Litnigg to.

pa rejoyd when he come
and spid the mars Like Candles smut
on the bed room Cornes

Than Ma had Gerge Edie Peg so on
but no ANGEL.

*

Edie was kind
Gerge fot
Peg the devel Mishif
Hennr did:

when 2 i nerle did
i dont remberer

when the Docter come for Hene Harry
Peg stol the Doters hat
but she was Cott:
he being Old whit berd Like the Old King
smild angerlie
give me

Ma sad ile Tan you my girl
pa a way
and she wolop Pege after

Than pa come in he sade wer is harry
and Ma cride
he past over

and pa Lift his Ey on to HEVEN
its a Merce

*

all so 2 older:

Ma sad you woned
for the ANGEL blesing
she rade the BIBLE Storres in bed

Adam Eve Nore
Mose in the baskip
Joseph my name
the buring firy firnes
and the ritig on the Wall
Like at the fish Mogres winnod.
so i ha a game
in Mas cubed

i was Norrer
in the Smells
and the flod out
and i wot to Lagh all Trebling
but i did not

Than Ma buss in and Shew me.

*

pas a venters at Sea as folos
he got in a Tempes at the Cape of Hop
a gret Wale bang his bote at Green Land
and a man eten
pa fell to
Save by a rope
at the noth Pole he saw the Ora Bols sky Liths
at Mala he Lay in fever 9 days
and Leches on his hed
in Arab the King gave a cammel Ey to swolaw

and other:

his presens we a big Mask of the Affic devel
Toy animels of Eximo
and a prete Tin box of Egit for Ma

CHRISTOPHER REID

My Spirit Will Not Haunt the Mound

My spirit will not haunt the mound
    Above my breast,
But travel, memory-possessed,
To where my tremulous being found
    Life largest, best.

My phantom-footed shape will go
    When nightfall grays
Hither and thither along the ways
I and another used to know
    In backward days.

And there you'll find me, if a jot
    You still should care
For me, and for my curious air;
If otherwise, then I shall not,
    For you, be there.

THOMAS HARDY

On a Midsummer Eve

I idly cut a parsley stalk,
And blew therein towards the moon;
I had not thought what ghosts would walk
With shivering footsteps to my tune.

I went, and knelt, and scooped my hand
As if to drink, into the brook,
And a faint figure seemed to stand
Above me, with the bygone look.

I lipped rough rhymes of chance, not choice,
I thought not what my words might be;
There came into my ear a voice
That turned a tenderer verse for me.

THOMAS HARDY

'The Wind – tapped like a tired Man'

The Wind – tapped like a tired Man –
And like a Host – 'Come in'
I boldly answered – entered then
My Residence within

A Rapid – footless Guest –
To offer whom a Chair
Were as impossible as hand
A Sofa to the Air –

No Bone had He to bind Him –
His Speech was like the Push
Of numerous Humming Birds at once
From a superior Bush –

His Countenance – a Billow –
His Fingers, as He passed
Let go a music – as of tunes
Blown tremulous in Glass –

He visited – still flitting –
Then like a timid Man
Again, He tapped – 'twas flurriedly –
And I became alone –

EMILY DICKINSON

Prayer Before Birth

I am not yet born; O hear me.
Let not the bloodsucking bat or the rat or the
                                              stoat or the
  club-footed ghoul come near me.

I am not yet born, console me.
I fear that the human race may with tall walls
                                              wall me,
  with strong drugs dope me, with wise lies lure
                                              me,
    on black racks rack me, in blood-baths roll
                                              me.

I am not yet born; provide me
With water to dandle me, grass to grow for me,
                                              trees to talk
  to me, sky to sing to me, birds and a white
                                              light
  in the back of my mind to guide me.

I am not yet born; forgive me
For the sins that in me the world shall commit,
                                              my words
  when they speak me, my thoughts when they
                                              think me,
  my treason engendered by traitors beyond
                                              me,
    my life when they murder by means of my
    hands, my death when they live me.

I am not yet born; rehearse me
In the parts I must play and the cues I must take
when
old men lecture me, bureaucrats hector me,
mountains
frown at me, lovers laugh at me, the white
waves call me to folly and the desert calls
me to doom and the beggar refuses
my gift and my children curse me.

I am not yet born; O hear me,
Let not the man who is beast or who thinks he is
God
come near me.

I am not yet born; O fill me
With strength against those who would freeze my
humanity, would dragoon me into a lethal
automaton,
would make me a cog in a machine, a thing
with
one face, a thing, and against all those
who would dissipate my entirety, would
blow me like thistledown hither and
thither or hither and thither
like water held in the
hands would spill me.

Let them not make me a stone and let them not
spill me.

Otherwise kill me.

LOUIS MACNEICE

De

I am a bairn.
I am de.
I am in de.

Du is a bairn. Du stands at da hert
O da settlement. Dy feet ir bare,
stuck/mud   Dir dirty, klestered wi gutter.
clothes   Dy body is cled wi coorse cloot.
Da reek o baests is apo dy skyn.
Hit is dy smell.
smell   Du fingers da waa o dy hame,
Near da daek quhar da sentry staands.
enclosure/built   It's a big roon crø, biggit be haand,
soil/grass   Møld underfit an owrehead girss.
dirty   Du touches dy hair, hit's aggelt an lang.
let alone   Du's never seen dy face, forbye atill da
Faces o dy bridders an dy sisters; du døsna ken
If du is 'beautiful' – but du feels it.

Da kennin is in de.
Du døsna seek 'knowledge'.
Feet in da gutter, du belangs.

ROBERT ALAN JAMIESON

Devil and the Princess

devil   Mister Winkler   Winkler oh
coocoorico
the gal is gone
awake me
at the   wake me look a hole
the gal was gone

ANON

Slegging

You Worthless

Telltale tit
yer mammy cant knit
yer daddy never goes to bed
without a dummy tit

*

Proddy proddy on the wall
penny bun to feed yiz all
a farthing candle to give yiz light
to read the Bible on Saturday night

*

Yer auld man's a dirty auld man
he washes his face in the frying pan
he combs his hair with the leg of a chair
yer auld man's a dirty auld man

*

in the path

You worthless Becca Watson
you worthless Becca Watson
you worthless Becca Watson
you ought to been ashame
them write yo name an trow it a pass
them write yo name an trow it a pass
them write yo name an trow it a pass
you ought to been ashame

ANON

Man United

Man United
are shortsighted
tra la la lalaLA

they wear glasses
on their asses
tra la la lalaLA

ANON

On Spies

Spies you are lights in state, but of base stuffe,
Who, when you have burnt your selves downe to
    the snuffe,
Stinke, and are throwne away. End faire enough.

BEN JONSON

Green Grass

Here we're set upon the green grass
green grass   green grass
here we're set upon the green grass
as green as any flower

Mary Murrays stole away
stole away   stole away
Mary Murrays stole away
stole away   stole away

Its well seen by her pale face
pale face   pale face
its well seen by her pale face
she may turn her face to the wall

ANON

An Epigram on Scolding

Great folks are of a finer mould;
Lord! how politely they can scold;
While a coarse English tongue will itch,
For whore and rogue; and dog and bitch.

JONATHAN SWIFT

Grasshopper is a Burden

Desire has failed, desire has failed
and the critical grasshopper
has come down on the heart in a burden of
    locusts
and stripped it bare.

D. H. LAWRENCE

Bryan O'Lynn

Bryan O'Lynn was a Dutchman born
his shoes were hemp and his stockings were yarn
his shoes were hemp and the water got in
its damp to my feet said Bryan O'Lynn
      all to my tooth a laugh a lum lee
      Bryan a ranter and a rover
      and a bone of my stover
      brew screw rivet and tin
its damp to my feet said Bryan O'Lynn

Bryan O'Lynn had no boots to put on
but two calves skins with the hair all gone
they were split at the side and the water ran in
I must wear wet feet said Bryan O'Lynn

Bryan O'Lynn has a hunting gone
a bridle of mouse tails has he put on
the bridle broke and the horse ran away
I'm not over well bridled said Bryan today

hedgehog

Bryan O'Lynn has a hunting gone
a saddle of urchin skins he put on
the urchins prickles were sharp as a pin
I've got a sore seat said Bryan O'Lynn

Bryan O'Lynns daughter sat on the stair
O father I fancy I'm wondrous fair!
the stairs they broke and the maid fell in
youre fair enough now said Bryan O'Lynn

Bryan O'Lynn his wife and his mother
they all fell into the fire together
ow yow! said the uppermost I've a hot skin
its hotter below said Bryan O'Lynn

ANON

On Mr Dryden, Renegade

Scorning religion all thy lifetime past,
And now embracing popery at last,
Is like thyself — and what thou'st done before
Defying wife and marrying a whore.
Alas! how leering heretics will laugh
To see a gray old hedge bird caught with chaff.
A poet, too, from great heroic themes
And inspiration, fallen to dreaming dreams.
But this the priests will get by thee at least
That if they mend thee, miracles are not ceased.
For 'tis not more to cure the lame and blind,
Than heal an impious ulcerated mind.
This if they do, and give thee but a grain
Of common honesty, or common shame,
Twill be more credit to their cause, I grant,
Than 'twould to make another man a saint.
But thou no party ever shalt adorn,
To thy own shame and nature's scandal borne:
All shun alike thy ugly outward part,
Whilst none have right or title to thy heart.
Resolved to stand and constant to the time,
Fixed in thy lewdness, settled in thy crime.
Whilst Moses with the Israelites abode,
Thou seemdst content to worship Moses' God:
But since he went and since thy master fell,
Thou foundst a golden calf would do as well.
And when another Moses shall arise
Once more I know thou'lt rub and clear thy eyes,
And turn to be an Israelite again,
For when the play is done and finished clean,
What should the poet do but shift the scene?

APHRA BEHN

Harpkin

Harpkin gaed up t'the hill
and blew his horn loud an shrill
and by came Fin

what for stand you there? quo Fin
spying the weather quo Harpkin

what for had you yur staff on yur shouther? quo
    Fin
to haud the cauld frae me quo Harpkin

drive

little cauld will that haud frae you quo Fin
as little will it win thraw me quo Harpkin

I came by yur door quo Fin
it lay in yur road quo Harpkin

yur dog barkit at me quo Fin
it's his use and custom quo Harpkin

I flang a stane at him quo Fin
I'd rather it had been a bane quo Harpkin

yur wife's lichter quo Fin
she'll clim the brae brichter quo Harpkin

of a braw lad bairn quo Fin
there'll be the more men for the king's wars quo
    Harpkin

straw

two stooks

there's a strae at yur beard quo Fin
I'd rather it had been a thrave quo Harpkin

the ox is eating at it quo Fin
if the ox were i' the water quo Harpkin

and the water were frozen quo Fin

sledge-hammer   and the smith and his fore-hammer at it quo
     Harpkin

and the smith were dead quo Fin
and another in his stead quo Harpkin

giff gaff quo Fin

dregs   yur mou's fou a draff quo Harpkin

ANON

Trees and Plants and Rivers

Aspens

All day and night, save winter, every weather,
Above the inn, the smithy, and the shop,
The aspens at the cross-roads talk together
Of rain, until their last leaves fall from the top.

Out of the blacksmith's cavern comes the ringing
Of hammer, shoe, and anvil; out of the inn
The clink, the hum, the roar, the random singing—
The sounds that for these fifty years have been.

The whisper of the aspens is not drowned,
And over lightless pane and footless road,
Empty as sky, with every other sound
Not ceasing, calls their ghosts from their abode,

A silent smithy, a silent inn, nor fails
In the bare moonlight or the thick-furred gloom,
In tempest or the night of nightingales,
To turn the cross-roads to a ghostly room.

And it would be the same were no house near.
Over all sorts of weather, men, and times,
Aspens must shake their leaves and men may
      hear
But need not listen, more than to my rhymes.

Whatever wind blows, while they and I have
      leaves
We cannot other than an aspen be
That ceaselessly, unreasonably grieves,
Or so men think who like a different tree.

EDWARD THOMAS

Sunny Gale

turkey cocks	The trees were like bubblyjocks
gold	In the wild gowd wind,
	The way that they fattened
	And the way that they thinned
commotion	And the stramash they made.
tops/stretching	Noo wi' taps streekit oot,
easing	Eisenin' into the sun,
	Their leafs scrauchin'; and syne
	Swallin' back on the grun'
lost	And tint in the shade.
always	But aye they raxed oot
sky	Whustlin' heich in the lift
bent	And aye loutit back
odd	Wi' orra leafs left adrift
	In their shaddaws' black whirlpools
one	Round my lugs the a'e meenit
	In squabbles o' green
misshapen	And the neist in a wan doze
	Fer awa' they'd be seen
half-smothered in soil	Or half-smoored i' the mools.

HUGH MACDIARMID

Bare Almond-Trees

Wet almond-trees, in the rain,
Like iron sticking grimly out of earth;
Black almond trunks, in the rain,
Like iron implements twisted, hideous, out of the
    earth,
Out of the deep, soft fledge of Sicilian winter-
    green,
Earth-grass uneatable,
Almond trunks curving blackly, iron-dark,
    climbing the slopes.

Almond-tree, beneath the terrace rail,
Black, rusted, iron trunk,
You have welded your thin stems finer,
Like steel, like sensitive steel in the air,
Grey, lavender, sensitive steel, curving thinly and
    brittly up in a parabola.
What are you doing in the December rain?
Have you a strange electric sensitiveness in your
    steel tips?
Do you feel the air for electric influences
Like some strange magnetic apparatus?
Do you take in messages, in some strange code,
From heaven's wolfish, wandering electricity, that
    prowls so constantly round Etna?
Do you take the whisper of sulphur from the air?
Do you hear the chemical accents of the sun?
Do you telephone the roar of the waters over the
    earth?
And from all this, do you make calculations?

Sicily, December's Sicily in a mass of rain
With iron branching blackly, rusted like old,
    twisted implements
And brandishing and stooping over earth's
    wintry fledge, climbing the slopes
Of uneatable soft green!

Taormina

D. H. LAWRENCE

Bare Fig-Trees

Fig-trees, weird fig-trees
Made of thick smooth silver,
Made of sweet, untarnished silver in the sea-
    southern air –
I say untarnished, but I mean opaque –
Thick, smooth-fleshed silver, dull only as human
    limbs are dull
With the life-lustre,
Nude with the dim light of full, healthy life
That is always half-dark,
And suave like passion-flower petals,
Like passion-flowers,
With the half-secret gleam of a passion-flower
    hanging from the rock,
Great, complicated, nude fig-tree, stemless
    flower-mesh,
Flowerily naked in flesh, and giving off hues of
    life.

Rather like an octopus, but strange and sweet-
    myriad-limbed octopus;
Like a nude, like a rock-living, sweet-fleshed sea-
    anemone,
Flourishing from the rock in a mysterious
    arrogance.

Let me sit down beneath the many-branching
    candelabrum
That lives upon this rock
And laugh at Time, and laugh at dull Eternity,
And make a joke of stale Infinity,
Within the flesh-scent of this wicked tree,
That has kept so many secrets up its sleeve,
And has been laughing through so many ages
At man and his uncomfortablenesses,
And his attempt to assure himself that what is so
    is not so,
Up its sleeve.

Let me sit down beneath this many-branching
    candelabrum,
The Jewish seven-branched, tallow-stinking
    candlestick kicked over the cliff
And all its tallow righteousness got rid of,
And let me notice it behave itself.

And watch it putting forth each time to heaven,
Each time straight to heaven,
With marvellous naked assurance each single
    twig.
Each one setting off straight to the sky
As if it were the leader, the main-stem, the
    forerunner,
Intent to hold the candle of the sun upon its
    socket-tip,
It alone.

Every young twig
No sooner issued sideways from the thigh of his
    predecessor
Than off he starts without a qualm
To hold the one and only lighted candle of the
    sun in his socket-tip.
He casually gives birth to another young bud
    from his thigh,
Which at once sets off to be the one and only,
And hold the lighted candle of the sun.

Oh many-branching candelabrum, oh strange up-
    starting fig-tree,
Oh weird Demos, where every twig is the arch
    twig,
Each imperiously over-equal to each, equality
    over-reaching itself
Like the snakes on Medusa's head,
Oh naked fig-tree!

Still, no doubt every one of you can be the sun-
    socket as well as every other of you.
Demos, Demos, Demos!
Demon, too,
Wicked fig-tree, equality puzzle, with your self-
    conscious secret fruits.

                                        Taormina

                    D. H. LAWRENCE

Birches

When I see birches bend to left and right
Across the lines of straighter darker trees,
I like to think some boy's been swinging them.
But swinging doesn't bend them down to stay

As ice storms do. Often you must have seen
   them
Loaded with ice a sunny winter morning
After a rain. They click upon themselves
As the breeze rises, and turn many-colored
As the stir cracks and crazes their enamel.
Soon the sun's warmth makes them shed crystal
   shells
Shattering and avalanching on the snow crust —
Such heaps of broken glass to sweep away
You'd think the inner dome of heaven had fallen.
They are dragged to the withered bracken by the
   load,
And they seem not to break; though once they
   are bowed
So low for long, they never right themselves:
You may see their trunks arching in the woods
Years afterwards, trailing their leaves on the
   ground
Like girls on hands and knees that throw their
   hair
Before them over their heads to dry in the sun.
But I was going to say when Truth broke in
With all her matter of fact about the ice storm,
I should prefer to have some boy bend them
As he went out and in to fetch the cows —
Some boy too far from town to learn baseball,
Whose only play was what he found himself,
Summer or winter, and could play alone.
One by one he subdued his father's trees
By riding them down over and over again
Until he took the stiffness out of them,
And not one but hung limp, not one was left
For him to conquer. He learned all there was
To learn about not launching out too soon
And so not carrying the tree away
Clear to the ground. He always kept his poise
To the top branches, climbing carefully

With the same pains you use to fill a cup
Up to the brim, and even above the brim.
Then he flung outward, feet first, with a swish,
Kicking his way down through the air to the
    ground.
So was I once myself a swinger of birches.
And so I dream of going back to be.
It's when I'm weary of considerations,
And life is too much like a pathless wood
Where your face burns and tickles with the
    cobwebs
Broken across it, and one eye is weeping
From a twig's having lashed across it open.
I'd like to get away from earth awhile
And then come back to it and begin over.
May no fate willfully misunderstand me
And half grant what I wish and snatch me away
Not to return. Earth's the right place for love:
I don't know where it's likely to go better.
I'd like to go by climbing a birch tree,
And climb black branches up a snow-white trunk
Toward heaven, till the tree could bear no more,
But dipped its top and set me down again.
That would be good both going and coming
    back.
One could do worse than be a swinger of birches.

ROBERT FROST

Felling a Tree

The surge of spirit that goes with using an axe,
The first heat – and calming down till the stiff
    back's
Unease passed, and the hot moisture came on
    body.

There under banks of Dane and Roman with the
    golden
Imperial coloured flower, whose name is lost to
    me –
Hewing the trunk desperately with upward
    strokes;
Seeing the chips fly – (it was at shoulder height,
    the trunk)
The green go, and the white appear –
Who should have been making music, but this
    had to be done
To earn a cottage shelter, and milk, and a little
    bread:
To right a body, beautiful as water and honour
    could make one –
And like the soldier lithe of body in the foremost
    rank
I stood there, muscle stiff, free of arm, working
    out fear.
Glad it was the ash tree's hardness not of the
    oaks', of the iron oak.
Sweat dripped from me – but there was no stay
    and the echoing bank
Sent back sharp sounds of hacking and of true
    straight woodcraft.
Some Roman from the pinewood caught memory
    and laughed.
Hit, crack and false aim, echoed from the
    amphitheatre
Of what was Rome before Romulus drew
    shoulder of Remus
Nearer his own – or Fabius won his salvation of
    victories.
In resting I thought of the hidden farm and
    Rome's hidden mild yoke
Still on the Gloucester heart strong after love's
    fill of centuries,

For all the happy, or the quiet, Severn or Leadon
    streams.
Pondered on music's deep truth, poetry's form or
    metre,
Rested – and took a thought and struck onward
    again,
Who had frozen by Chaulnes out of all caring of
    pain –
Learnt Roman fortitude at Laventie or Ypres,
Saw bright edge bury dull in the beautiful wood,
Touched splinters so wonderful – half through
    and soon to come down
From that ledge of rock under harebell, the
    yellow flower – the pinewood's crown.
Four inches more – and I should hear the crash
    and great thunder
Of an ash Crickley had loved for a century, and
    kept her own.
Thoughts of soldier and musician gathered to me
The desire of conquest ran in my blood, went
    through me –
There was a battle in my spirit and my blood
    shared it,
Maisemore – and Gloucester – bred me, and
    Cotswold reared it,
This great tree standing nobly in the July's day
    full light
Nearly to fall – my courage broke – and gathered
    – my breath feared it,
My heart – and again I struck, again the splinters
    and steel glinters
Dazzled my eyes – and the pain and the
    desperation and near victory
Carried me onwards – there were exultations and
    mockings sunward
Sheer courage, as of boat sailings in equinoctial
    unsafe squalls,

Stiffened my virtue, and the thing was done. No.
    Dropped my body,
The axe dropped – for a minute, taking breath,
    and gathering the greedy
Courage – looking for rest to the farm and grey
    loose-piled walls,
Rising like Troilus to the first word of 'Ready',
The last desperate onslaught – took the two
    inches of too steady
Trunk – on the rock edge it lurched, threatening
    my labouring life
(Nearly on me). Like Trafalgar's own sails
    imperiously moving to defeat
Across the wide sky unexpected glided and the
    high bank's pines and fell straight
Lower and lower till the crashing of the fellow
    trees made strife.
The thud of earth, and the full tree lying low in
    state,
With all its glory of life and sap quick in the
    veins . . .
Such beauty, for the farm fires and heat against
    chilly rains,
Golden glows in the kitchen from what a century
    made great . . .

The axe fell from my hand, and I was proud of
    my hand,
Crickley forgave, for her nobleness, the common
    fate of trees
As noble or more noble, the oak, the elm that is
    treacherous,
But dear for her cherishing to this beloved and
    this rocky land.
Over above all world there, in a tired glory
    swerved there,
To a fall, the tree that for long had watched
    Wales glow strong,

Seen Severn, and farm, and Brecon, Black
    Mountains times without reckon.
And tomorrow would be fuel for the bright
    kitchen – for brown tea, against cold night.

    IVOR GURNEY

Yorkshire Forest Sign

FIRE – DON'T YOU START ONE

    ANON

'Says Tweed tae Till'

Says Tweed tae Till
makes/quiet   what gars ye rin sae still?

says Till tae Tweed
though ye rin wi' speed
and I rin slaw
each   for ae man that ye droon
I droon twa

    ANON

from The Bothie of Tober-Na-Vuolich, III

There is a stream, I name not its name, let
    inquisitive tourist
Hunt it, and make it a lion, and get it at last into
    guide-books,
Springing far off from a loch unexplored in the
    folds of great mountains,

Falling two miles through rowan and stunted
  alder, enveloped
Then for four more in a forest of pine, where
  broad and ample
Spreads, to convey it, the glen with heathery
  slopes on both sides:
Broad and fair the stream, with occasional falls
  and narrows;
But, where the glen of its course approaches the
  vale of the river,
Met and blocked by a huge interposing mass of
  granite,
Scarce by a channel deep-cut, raging up, and
  raging onward,
Forces its flood through a passage so narrow a
  lady would step it.
There, across the great rocky wharves, a wooden
  bridge goes,
Carrying a path to the forest; below, three
  hundred yards, say,
Lower in level some twenty-five feet, through
  flats of shingle,
Stepping-stones and a cart-track cross in the open
  valley.
  But in the interval here the boiling, pent-up
  water
Frees itself by a final descent, attaining a basin,
Ten feet wide and eighteen long with whiteness
  and fury
Occupied partly, but mostly pellucid, pure, a
  mirror;
Beautiful there for the colour derived from green
  rocks under;
Beautiful, most of all, where beads of foam
  uprising
Mingle their clouds of white with the delicate hue
  of the stillness.

Cliff over cliff for its sides, with rowan and
   pendent birch boughs,
Here it lies, unthought of above at the bridge and
   pathway,
Still more enclosed from below by wood and
   rocky projection.
You are shut in, left alone with yourself and
   perfection of water,
Hid on all sides, left alone with yourself and the
   goddess of bathing.
   Here, the pride of the plunger, you stride the
   fall and clear it;
Here, the delight of the bather, you roll in
   beaded sparklings,
Here into pure green depth drop down from lofty
   ledges.

ARTHUR HUGH CLOUGH

The Clote

Water-Lily

O zummer clote! when the brook's a-gliden
   So slow an' smooth down his zedgy bed,
Upon thy broad leaves so seäfe a-riden
   The water's top wi' thy yollow head,
      By alder's heads, O,
      An' bulrush beds, O,
Thou then dost float, goolden zummer clote!

The grey-bough'd withy's a-leänen lowly
   Above the water thy leaves do hide;
The benden bulrush, a-swaÿen slowly,
   Do skirt in zummer thy river's zide;
      An' perch in shoals, O,
      Do vill the holes, O,
Where thou dost float, goolden zummer clote!

Oh! when thy brook-drinken flow'r's a-blowen,
   The burnen zummer's a-zetten in;
The time o' greenness, the time o' mowen,
    When in the hay-vield, wi' zunburnt skin,
       The vo'k do drink, O,
       Upon the brink, O,
Where thou dost float, goolden zummer clote!

Wi' eärms a-spreaden an' cheäks a-blowen,
   How proud wer I when I vu'st could zwim
Athirt the pleäce where thou bist a-growen,
    Wi' thy long more vrom the bottom dim;
       While cows, knee-high, O,
       In brook, wer nigh, O,
Where thou dost float, goolden zummer clote!

Ov all the brooks drough the meäds a-winden,
   Ov all the meäds by a river's brim,
There's nwone so feäir o' my own heart's vinden,
    As where the maïdens do zee thee zwim,
       An' stan' to teäke, O,
       Wi' long-stemm'd reäke, O,
Thy flow'r afloat, goolden zummer clote!

WILLIAM BARNES

root   (margin note)

Thistles

Against the rubber tongues of cows and the
   hoeing hands of men
Thistles spike the summer air
Or crackle open under a blue-black pressure.

Every one a revengeful burst
Of resurrection, a grasped fistful
Of splintered weapons and Icelandic frost thrust
  up

From the underground stain of a decayed Viking.
They are like pale hair and the gutturals of
   dialects.
Every one manages a plume of blood.

Then they grow grey, like men.
Mown down, it is a feud. Their sons appear,
Stiff with weapons, fighting back over the same
   ground.

    TED HUGHES

Tall Nettles

Tall nettles cover up, as they have done
These many springs, the rusty harrow, the plough
Long worn out, and the roller made of stone:
Only the elm butt tops the nettles now.

This corner of the farmyard I like most:
As well as any bloom upon a flower
I like the dust on the nettles, never lost
Except to prove the sweetness of a shower.

    EDWARD THOMAS

Stir Among the Dead

Patch-Shaneen

Shaneen and Maurya Prendergast
Lived west in Carnareagh,
And they'd a cur-dog, cabbage plot,
A goat, and cock of hay.

He was five foot one or two,
Herself was four foot ten,
And he went travelling asking meal
Above through Caragh Glen.

edible seaweed   She'd pick her bag of carrageen
periwinkles   Or perries through the surf,
Or loan an ass of Foxy Jim
To fetch her creel of turf.

All Souls'   Till on one windy Samhain night,
When there's stir among the dead,
He found her perished, stiff and stark,
Beside him in the bed.

And now when Shaneen travels far
From Droum to Ballyhyre
The women lay him sacks or straw,
Beside the seed of fire.

And when the grey cocks crow and flap,
And winds are in the sky,
'Oh, Maurya, Maurya, are you dead?'
You'll hear Patch-Shaneen cry.

J. M. SYNGE

'Under the Light, yet under'

Under the Light, yet under,
Under the Grass and the Dirt,
Under the Beetle's Cellar
Under the Clover's Root,

Further than Arm could stretch
Were it Giant long,
Further than Sunshine could
Were the Day Year long,

Over the Light, yet over,
Over the Arc of the Bird —
Over the Comet's chimney —
Over the Cubit's Head,

Further than Guess can gallop
Further than riddle ride —
Oh for a Disc to the Distance
Between Ourselves and the Dead!

EMILY DICKINSON

Friends Beyond

William Dewy, Tranter Reuben, Farmer Ledlow
   late at plough,
      Robert's kin, and John's, and Ned's,
And the Squire, and Lady Susan, lie in Mellstock
   churchyard now!

'Gone,' I call them, gone for good, that group of
    local hearts and heads;
        Yet at mothy curfew-tide,
And at midnight when the noon-heat breathes it
    back from walls and leads,

They've a way of whispering to me – fellow-
    wight who yet abide –
        In the muted, measured note
Of a ripple under archways, or a lone cave's
dripping water   stillicide:

'We have triumphed: this achievement turns the
    bane to antidote,
        Unsuccesses to success,
Many thought-worn eves and morrows to a
    morrow free of thought.

'No more need we corn and clothing, feel of old
    terrestrial stress;
        Child detraction stirs no sigh;
Fear of death has even bygone us: death gave all
    that we possess.'

W.D. – 'Ye mid burn the old bass-viol that I set
    such value by.'
Squire. – 'You may hold the manse in fee,
    You may wed my spouse, may let my
    children's memory of me die.'

Lady S. – 'You may have my rich brocades, my
    laces; take each household key;
        Ransack coffer, desk, bureau;
    Quiz the few poor treasures hid there, con
    the letters kept by me.'

wild mustard
granary bins

Far. – 'Ye mid zell my favourite heifer, ye mid let
    the charlock grow,
        Foul the grinterns, give up thrift.'
Far. Wife. – 'If ye break my best blue china,
    children, I shan't care or ho.'

All. – 'We've no wish to hear the tidings, how
    the people's fortunes shift;
        What your daily doings are;
     Who are wedded, born, divided; if your lives
    beat slow or swift.

'Curious not the least are we if our intents you
    make or mar,
        If you quire to our old tune,
If the City stage still passes, if the weirs still roar
    afar.'

– Thus, with very gods' composure, freed those
    crosses late and soon
        Which, in life, the Trine allow
(Why, none witteth), and ignoring all that haps
    beneath the moon,

William Dewy, Tranter Reuben, Farmer Ledlow
    late at plough,
        Robert's kin, and John's, and Ned's,
And the Squire, and Lady Susan, murmur mildly
    to me now.

THOMAS HARDY

Voices from Things Growing
in a Churchyard

These flowers are I, poor Fanny Hurd,
            Sir or Madam,
A little girl here sepultured.
Once I flit-fluttered like a bird
Above the grass, as now I wave
In daisy shapes above my grave,
            All day cheerily,
            All night eerily!

— I am one Bachelor Bowring, 'Gent',
            Sir or Madam;
In shingled oak my bones were pent;
Hence more than a hundred years I spent
In my feat of change from a coffin-thrall
To a dancer in green as leaves on a wall,
            All day cheerily,
            All night eerily!

— I, these berries of juice and gloss,
            Sir or Madam,
Am clean forgotten as Thomas Voss;
Thin-urned, I have burrowed away from the
    moss
That covers my sod, and have entered this yew,
And turned to clusters ruddy of view,
            All day cheerily,
            All night eerily!

– The Lady Gertrude, proud, high-bred,
      Sir or Madam,
Am I – this laurel that shades your head;
Into its veins I have stilly sped,
And made them of me; and my leaves now shine,
As did my satins superfine,
      All day cheerily,
      All night eerily!

– I, who as innocent withwind climb,
      Sir or Madam,
Am one Eve Greensleeves, in olden time
Kissed by men from many a clime,
Beneath sun, stars, in blaze, in breeze,
As now by glowworms and by bees,
      All day cheerily,
      All night eerily!

– I'm old Squire Audeley Grey, who grew,
      Sir or Madam,
Aweary of life, and in scorn withdrew;
Till anon I clambered up anew
As ivy-green, when my ache was stayed,
And in that attire I have longtime gayed
      All day cheerily,
      All night eerily!

– And so these maskers breathe to each
      Sir or Madam
Who lingers there, and their lively speech
Affords an interpreter much to teach,
As their murmurous accents seem to come
Thence hitheraround in a radiant hum,
      All day cheerily,
      All night eerily!

THOMAS HARDY

Lying Awake

You, Morningtide Star, now are steady-eyed,
    over the east,
        I know it as if I saw you;
You, Beeches, engrave on the sky your thin twigs,
    even the least;
        Had I paper and pencil I'd draw you.

You, Meadow, are white with your counterpane
    cover of dew,
        I see it as if I were there;
You, Churchyard, are lightening faint from the
    shade of the yew,
        The names creeping out everywhere.

THOMAS HARDY

Death of an Old Lady

At five in the morning there were grey voices
Calling three times through the dank fields;
The ground fell away beyond the voices
Forty long years to the wrinkled lough
That had given a child one shining glimpse
Of a boat so big it was named Titanic.

Named or called? For a name is a call —
Shipyard voices at five in the morning,
As now for this old tired lady who sails
Towards her own iceberg calm and slow;
We hardly hear the screws, we hardly
Can think her back her four score years.

They called and ceased. Later the night nurse
Handed over, the day went down
To the sea in a ship, it was grey April,
The daffodils in her garden waited
To make her a wreath, the iceberg waited;
At eight in the evening the ship went down.

LOUIS MACNEICE

The Wold Clock

The wold clock's feäce is still in pleäce,
Wi' hands a-stealen round,
His bob do swing an' bell do ring,
As when I heärd his sound,
A-leäven hwome, so long a-gone,
An' left en there, a-ticken on.

Noo doust do clog, noo rust uncog
His wheels to keep em still,
Noo blow ha' vell to crack his bell
That still do ringle shrill.
I wish that I'd a-gone so well
'S the clock's wold bob, an' wheels, an' bell.

Who now do wind his chaïn, a-twin'd
As he do run his hours,
Or meäke a gloss to sheen across
His door, wi' goolden flow'rs,
Since he've a-sounded out the last
Still hours our dear good mother pass'd?

WILLIAM BARNES

has fallen

broken rainbow

The Watergaw

*one wet early evening/cold
spell after sheep-shearing
rare*

shivering

beyond the downpour

Ae weet forenicht i' the yow-trummle
I saw yon antrin thing,
A watergaw wi' its chitterin' licht
Ayont the on-ding;
An' I thocht o' the last wild look ye gied
Afore ye deed!

smoke/skylark's

There was nae reek i' the laverock's hoose
That nicht – an' nane i' mine;
But I hae thocht o' that foolish licht
Ever sin' syne;
An' I think that mebbe at last I ken
What your look meant then.

HUGH MACDIARMID

Farmer's Death

For Edwin Muir

Ke-uk, ke-uk, ke-uk, ki-kwaik,

retch

then

dig

The broon hens keckle and bouk,
And syne wi' their yalla beaks
For the reid worms houk.

The muckle white pig at the tail
O' the midden slotters and slorps,

quiet

wretched

But the auld ferm hoose is lown
And wae as a corpse.

The hen's een glitter like gless
As the worms gang twirlin' in,

inside

But there's never a move in by
And the windas are blin'.

Feathers turn fire i' the licht,
buttocks glitter　　The pig's doup skinkles like siller,
stale　　But the auld ferm hoose is waugh
Wi' the daith intill her.

panache　　Hen's cries are a panash in Heaven,
And a pig has the warld at its feet;
burly　　But wae for the hoose whaur a buirdly man
shrinks　　Crines in a windin' sheet.

HUGH MACDIARMID

The Ghost

I is the ghost of Stevey Fizzlegig,
　　If you'll believe me,
Who died for love of Sukey Swizzleswig,
　　It did so grieve me:
For nobody did never see,
　　In my life's time, that day when she
Did say, 'For Stevey Fizzlegig
　　I keres a single ha'penny'.
　　　　　　　Chorus. Oh! Oh! Oh!

Monument　　To Fag-lane, near the sign o' th' Morniment,
　　If you'll believe me,
To tell my love, oft'times, forlorn I went,
　　Which much did grieve me:
For there this Sukey Swizzleswig
stomachs　　　Baked faggots, maws and hogs-feet sells,
Jest oppersite Bess Frowzy's shed,
　　Who in it cat's and dog's meat sells.
　　　　　　　Chorus. Oh! Oh! Oh!

I could not work at all, through loving so,
   If you'll believe me,
Yet she preferred one they calls cussing Joe,
   Which much did grieve me,
'Cause he duz treat her oftentimes,
   And her out on a Sunday take;
And (though he'd better mind his work)

take a holiday   With her oft does St Monday make.
           Chorus. Oh! Oh! Oh!

Says I, 'Through Joe your scorn you throws at
                  me',
   If you'll believe me;
At them words she turns up her nose at me;
   How that did grieve me! ˙
But, when I sed 'I doubts he in
   A sartin place oft stops a gap',
She calls me sniv'ling cull, and then
   Gave each of these here chops a slap.
           Chorus. Oh! Oh! Oh!

Through this, when to my room up stairs I goes,
   If you'll believe me,
Says I, 'How full of thoughts and cares I grows,
   Which much does grieve me.'
And then, as I'd no chair, I fetched
   My master's little darter's stool,
And cried cause Suk had sarved me so,
   While I did off my garters pull.
           Chorus. Oh! Oh! Oh!

First, that they wouldn't eas'ly break I tries,
    If you'll believe me;
Next, one end of 'em round my neck I ties,
    And that did grieve me:
The stool I then did mount, and to
    A joist tied t'other end of 'em,
Then kicked the stool away, and swung
    Like our cuckoo-clock pendulum.
                        Chorus. Oh! Oh! Oh!

E'en when intarred she called me snotty fool,
    If you'll believe me,
Because my love was fur too hot to cool,
    And which did grieve me:
But, as I knows they're in the dark
    In Suk's back room, I'll whiz through air,
And in revenge I'll frighten 'em
    Until they sweat, nay, piss, through fear.
                        Chorus. Oh! Oh! Oh!

— O'BRIEN

The Cave of Making

(In Memoriam Louis MacNeice)

For this and for all enclosures like it the
                                archetype
    is Weland's Stithy, an antre
more private than a bedroom even, for neither
                                lovers nor
    maids are welcome, but without a
bedroom's secrets: from the Olivetti portable,
    the dictionaries (the very
best money can buy), the heaps of paper, it is
                                evident
    what must go on. Devoid of

flowers and family photographs, all is
                         subordinate
    here to a function, designed to
discourage daydreams – hence windows averted
                         from plausible
    videnda but admitting a light one
could mend a watch by – and to sharpen
                    hearing: reached by an
    outside staircase, domestic
noises and odors, the vast background of natural
  life are shut off. Here silence
is turned into objects.
                         I wish, Louis, I could have
                         shown it you
    while you were still in public,
and the house and garden: lover of women and
                         Donegal,
    from your perspective you'd notice
sights I overlook, and in turn take a scholar's
                         interest
    in facts I could tell you (for instance,
four miles to our east, at a wood palisade,
                         Carolingian
    Bavaria stopped, beyond it
unknowable nomads). Friends we became by
                         personal
    choice, but fate had already
made us neighbors. For Grammar we both
                         inherited
    good mongrel barbarian English
which never completely succumbed to the Roman
                         rhetoric
    or the Roman gravity, that nonsense
which stood none. Though neither of our dads,
                         like Horace's,
    wiped his nose on his forearm,

neither was porphyry-born, and our ancestors
                                    probably
    were among those plentiful subjects
it cost less money to murder. Born so, both of us
    became self-conscious at a moment
when locomotives were named after knights in
                                    Malory,
    Science to schoolboys was known as
Stinks, and the Manor still was politically
                                    numinous:
    both watched with mixed feelings
the sack of Silence, the churches empty, the
                                    cavalry
    go, the Cosmic Model
become German, and any faith, if we had it, in
                                    immanent
    virtue died. More than ever
life-out-there is goodly, miraculous, lovable,
    but we shan't, not since Stalin and Hitler,
trust ourselves ever again: we know that,
                                    subjectively,
    all is possible.
                    To you, though,
ever since, last Fall, you quietly slipped out of
                                    Granusion,
    our moist garden, into
the Country of Unconcern, no possibility
    matters. I wish you hadn't
caught that cold, but the dead we miss are easier
    to talk to: with those no longer
tensed by problems one cannot feel shy and,
                                    anyway,
    when playing cards or drinking
or pulling faces are out of the question, what else
                                    is there
    to do but talk to the voices

of conscience they have become? From now on,
                              as a visitor
    who needn't be met at the station,
your influence is welcome at any hour in my
                              ubity,
    especially here, where titles
from *Poems* to *The Burning Perch* offer proof
                              positive
    of the maker you were, with whom I
once collaborated, once at a weird Symposium
    exchanged winks as a juggins
went on about Alienation.
                              Who would, for
                              preference,
    be a bard in an oral culture,
obliged at drunken feasts to improvise a eulogy
    of some beefy illiterate burner,
giver of rings, or depend for bread on the moods
                              of a
    Baroque Prince, expected,
like his dwarf, to amuse? After all, it's rather a
                              privilege
    amid the affluent traffic
to serve this unpopular art which cannot be
                              turned into
    background noise for study
or hung as a status trophy by rising executives,
    cannot be 'done' like Venice
or abridged like Tolstoy, but stubbornly still
                              insists upon
    being read or ignored: our handful
of clients at least can rune. (It's heartless to
                              forget about
    the underdeveloped countries,
but a starving ear is as deaf as a suburban
                              optimist's:
    to stomachs only the Hindu

integers truthfully speak.) Our forerunners might
envy us
our remnant still able to listen:
as Nietzsche said they would, the *plebs* have got
steadily
denser, the *optimates*
quicker still on the uptake. (Today, even
Talleyrand
might seem a naïf: he had so
little to cope with.) I should like to become, if
possible,
a minor atlantic Goethe,
with his passion for weather and stones but
without his silliness
re the Cross: at times a bore, but,
while knowing Speech can at best, a shadow
echoing
the silent light, bear witness
to the Truth it is not, he wished it were, as the
Francophile
gaggle of pure songsters
are too vain to. We're not musicians: to stink of
Poetry
is unbecoming, and never
to be dull shows a lack of taste. Even a limerick
ought to be something a man of
honor, awaiting death from cancer or a firing
squad,
could read without contempt: (at
that frontier I wouldn't dare speak to anyone
in either a prophet's bellow
or a diplomat's whisper).
Seeing you know our
mystery
from the inside and therefore
how much, in our lonely dens, we need the
companionship
of our good dead, to give us

gloomy

comfort on dowly days when the self is a
                                        nonentity
    dumped on a mound of nothing,
to break the spell of our self-enchantment when
                                        lip-smacking
    imps of mawk and hooey
write with us what they will, you won't think me
                                        imposing if
    I ask you to stay at my elbow
until cocktail time: dear Shade, for your elegy
    I should have been able to manage
something more like you than this egocentric
                                        monologue,
    but accept it for friendship's sake.

    W. H. AUDEN

Work

Blacksmiths

black sooty	Swarte smeked smethes smatered with smoke
blows	drive me to deth with den of here dintes
	swich nois on nightes ne herd men never
workers	what knavene cry and clatering of knockes
snub-nosed changelings	the cammede kongons cryen after *Col Col*
	and blowen here bellewes that all here brain
	brestes
bursts	*huf puf* seith that on *haf paf* that other
tell many tales	they spitten and sprawlen and spellen many
	spelles
	they gnawen and gnacchen they grones togidere
keep themselves hot	and holden hem hote with here hard hamers
bull's hide are their leather aprons	of a bole hide ben here barm felles
legs are protected against the fiery sparks	here shankes ben shakeled for the fere flunderes
	hevy hameres they han that hard ben handled
steel anvil	stark strokes they striken on a steled stocke
crash in turn	*lus bus las das* rowten by rowe
put an end to	swiche dolful a dreme the devil it todrive
lengthens a little bit of iron and hammers a smaller bit twists them in two and touches a treble	the maister longeth a litil and lasheth a lesse
	twineth hem twein and toucheth a treble
	tik tak hic hac tiket taket tik tak
	lus bus lus das switch lif they leden
all who clothe horses in armour	alle clothemeres Christ hem give sorwe
burners of water they let no one sleep at night	may no man for brenwateres on night han his
	rest

ANON

A Digging Sing

Toady toady min yoself
min yoself make I plant me corn
plant me corn fe go plant me peas
plant me peas fe go kawt me gal
kawt me gal fe go show mumma
mumma de one a go tell me yes
puppa de one a go tell me no
toady toady min yoself
min yoself make I plant me corn

maize

green beans

ANON

Hammer-Song

Ee calazi
calazi calenia
tra la la
luff luff luff
ee calazi
cazee cazenia
tra la la la
luff luff luff
tra la lala la
luff luff luff
bout!

ANON

'You might easy know a doffer'

spinning-frame loader in linen mill

You might easy know a doffer
when she comes into town
with her long yella hair
instruments for picking out broken thread
apron
and her pickers hanging down
with her rubber tied before her
and her scraper in her hand
you might easy know a doffer
for she'll always get a man
oh she'll always get a man
you might easy know a doffer
for she'll always get a man

you might easy know a weaver
when she comes into town
with her old greasy hair
and her scissors hanging down
with a shawl around her shoulders
and a shuttle in her hand
you will easy know a weaver
for she'll never get a man
no she'll never get a man
no she'll never get a man
you will easy know a weaver
for she'll never get a man

ANON

Factory Workers' Song

Come carders an spinners an wayvers as weel
stop yor frames an yor jennies strip roller an
    creel
let yor lathes cease to swing an yor shuttles to fly
for theres gone through owd England a leaud
    battlecry –
Derry deawn!

Theyn turned eaut at Ratchda an Owdham an
    Shay
an th'Stalybridge lads are at Ash'n today
Fair Wage For Fair Work is the motto they'n
    chose
an what'll be th'upshot no mortal man knows –
Derry deawn!

Eaur mesthers are screwin eaur noses to th'dust
an if we don't strike we'n no maybe seen th'wust
they've cheeant up eaur bodies to slavery's wheel
and they'd sell if we'd let em eaur souls to the
    diel –
Derry deawn!

ANON

Street Cries

One a penny two a penny hot cross buns!
one a penny two a penny hot cross buns!

*

Maids I mend old pans and kettles
mend old pans or kettles O!

*

Muffins O! crumpets! muffins today!
crumpets O! muffins O! fresh today!

*

Clothes props! clothes props! I say good wives
clothes props all long and very strong today!

*

I have screens if you desire
to keep your buttey from the fire

*

Cherries a hapenny a stick
come and pick! come and pick!
cherries big as plums! who comes who comes?

*

One a penny poker
two a penny tongs
three a penny fire irons
HOT CROSS BUNS!

ANON

from The Vision of Piers Plowman

serfs too

Barones an burgeises and bondemen als
I seigh in this assemblee as ye shul here after

bakers/brewers/butchers
wool-weavers
toll-collectors
miners
all kind living
ditchers/diggers/work
pass

baxteres & brewesteres and bocheres manye
wollewebsteres and weueres of lynnen
taillours and tynkeres & tolleres in marketes
masons and mynours and many other craftes
of alkin libbyng laboreres lopen forthe somme
as dykers & deleueres that doon hire dedes ille
and dryuen forth the longe day with *Dieu save*
   Dame Emme!

servants
pork

cokes and hire knaves crieden *hote pies hote*!
goode gees and grys! go we dyne go we!
taverners vntil hem tolden the same

Alsace
digest

white wyn of Oseye and red wyn of Gascoigne
of the Ryn and of the Rochel the roste to defye!

WILLIAM LANGLAND

Stormalong!

Stormey's dead that good old man –
to my ay   Stormalong!
Stormey he is dead and gone
ay ay ay   Mister Stormalong!

Stormey's dead and gone to rest –
to my ay   Stormalong!
of all the skippers he was best –
ay ay ay   Mister Stormalong!

We dug his grave with a silver spade –
to my ay   Stormalong!
his shroud of softest silk was made
ay ay ay   Mister Stormalong!

I wish I was old Stormey's son –
to my ay   Stormalong!
I'd build a ship a thousand ton –
ay ay ay   Mister Stormalong!

I'd load her deep with wine and rum –
to my ay   Stormalong!
and all my shellbacks would have some –
ay ay ay   Mister Stormalong!

ANON

Omagh Post Office Rhyme

Augher Clogher Fivemiletown
circulate to Portadown

ANON

Butter Charm

Come butter come
come butter come
Peter stands at the gate
waiting for a buttered cake
come butter come

ANON

Poverty Knock

Poverty poverty knock!
me loom is a sayin all day
poverty poverty knock!
gaffer's too skinny to pay
poverty poverty knock!
keepin one eye on the clock
guzzle   ah know ah can guttle
when ah hear me shuttle
go: poverty poverty knock!

up every mornin at five
ah wonder that we keep alive
tired an yawnin on the cold mornin
it's back to the dreary old drive

oh dear we're goin t'be late
gaffer is stood at th'gate
we're out o'pocket our wages they're docket
we'll a' to buy grub on th'slate

an when our wages they'll bring
length of cloth   we're often short of a string
quarrelling   while we are fratchin wi gaffer for snatchin
we know to his brass he will cling

we've got to wet our own yarn
by dippin it into the tarn
it's wet an soggy an makes us feel groggy
an there's mice in that dirty old barn

oh dear me poor ead it sings
ah should have woven three strings
but threads are breakin and my back is achin
oh dear ah wish ah had wings

sometimes a shuttle flies out
gives some poor woman a clout
ther she lies bleedin but nobody's heedin
who's goin t'carry her out?

maintenance man   tuner should tackle me loom
eed rather sit on his bum
ees far too busy acourtin our Lizzie
an ah cannat get im to coom

Lizzie is so easy led
all think that ee teks her to bed
she allus was skinny now look at her pinny
it's just about time they was wed

poverty poverty knock!
me loom is asayin all day
poverty poverty knock!
gaffer's too skinny to pay
poverty poverty knock
keepin one eye on the clock
ah know ah can guttle
when ah hear me shuttle
go: poverty poverty knock!

     ANON

Shallow Brown

A Yankee ship came down the river
Shallow Shallow Brown
A Yankee ship came down the river
Shallow Shallow Brown
And who do you think was master of her?
Shallow Shallow Brown
And who do you think was master of her?
Shallow Shallow Brown

A Yankee mate and a limejuice skipper
Shallow Shallow Brown
A Yankee mate and a limejuice skipper
Shallow Shallow Brown
And what do you think they had for dinner?
Shallow Shallow Brown
And what do you think they had for dinner?
Shallow Shallow Brown
A parrot's tail and a monkey's liver
Shallow Shallow Brown
A parrot's tail and a monkey's liver
Shallow Shallow Brown

ANON

Linstead Market

fruit   Carry me ackee go a Linstead market
quarter   not a quatty wut sell
carry me ackee go a Linstead market
not a quatty wut sell
Lard wat a nite not a bite
wat a Satiday nite
Lard wat a nite not a bite
wat a Satiday nite

everybody come feel up feel up
not a quatty wut sell
everybody come feel up squeeze up
not a quatty wut sell
Lard wat a nite not a bite
wat a Satiday nite
Lard wat a nite not a bite
wat a Satiday nite

mek me call ih louder *ackee! ackee!*

stand

red an pretty dem tan

lady buy yu Sunday marnin brukfas

eat grand

rice an ackee nyam gran

Lard wat a nite not a bite

wat a Satiday nite

Lard wat a nite not a bite

wat a Satiday nite

kids get ill

all de pickney dem a linga linga

for what

fe weh dem mumma no bring

all de pickney dem a linga linga

fe weh dem mumma no bring

Lard wat a nite not a bite

wat a Satiday nite

Lard wat a nite not a bite

wat a Satiday nite

ANON

The Wee Falorie Man

mystery man

I am the wee falorie man

a rattling roving Irishman

I can do all that ever you can

for I am the wee falorie man

I have a sister Mary Ann

she washes her face in the frying pan

and out she goes to hunt for a man

I have a sister Mary Ann

I am a good ould working man
each day I carry a wee tin can
a large penny bap and a clipe of ham
I am a good ould working man

ANON

Bird Starver's Cry

Hi! shoo aller birds
shoo aller birds
shoo aller birds

Out of masters ground
into Tom Tuckers ground

Out of Tom Tuckers ground
into Tom Tinkers ground

Out of Tom Tinkers ground
into Luke Collins ground

Out of Luke Collins ground
into Bill Vaters ground

Hi! shoo aller birds
kraw! hoop!

ANON

In the Rain's Mouth

Weather Rhymes

Rainbow i'th'morning
shippers warning
rainbow at night
shippers delight

*

If there be a rainbow in the eve
it will rain and leave
but if there be a rainbow in the morrow
it will neither lend nor borrow

*

The ev'ning red and the morning gray
are the tokens of a bonny day

*

Winter's thunder
is the world's wonder

*

No weather is ill
if the wind be still

*

fog   a northern har
brings drought from far

*

Rain rain go to Spain
come again another day
when I brew and when I bake
I'll give you a figgy cake

*

When the wind is in the east
tis good for neither man nor beast
when the wind is in the south
it is in the rain's mouth

*

Clear moon
frost soon

*

sun or moon halo A far off brough
is a storm near enough

*

Wag ballock wag
neap tide a westerly wind an' a neeap fleead

*

Raan afoor seven
fair bi eleven

*

White frosts allus shite thersels

Entering the Language

Quoof

How often have I carried our family word
for the hot water bottle
to a strange bed,
as my father would juggle a red-hot half-brick
in an old sock
to his childhood settle.
I have taken it into so many lovely heads
or laid it between us like a sword.

An hotel room in New York City
with a girl who spoke hardly any English,
my hand on her breast
like the smouldering one-off spoor of the yeti
or some other shy beast
that has yet to enter the language.

PAUL MULDOON

The Ruined Maid

'O 'Melia, my dear, this does everything crown!
Who could have supposed I should meet you in
    Town?
And whence such fair garments, such pros-
    perity?' –
'O didn't you know I'd been ruined?' said she.

– 'You left us in tatters, without shoes or socks,
Tired of digging potatoes, and spudding up
    docks;
And now you've gay bracelets and bright feathers
    three!' –
'Yes: that's how we dress when we're ruined,'
    said she.

— 'At home in the barton you said "thee" and
  "thou",
And "thik oon", and "theäs oon", and "t'other";
  but now
Your talking quite fits 'ee for high compa-ny!' —
'Some polish is gained with one's ruin,' said she.

— 'Your hands were like paws then, your face
  blue and bleak
But now I'm bewitched by your delicate cheek,
And your little gloves fit as on any la-dy!'
'We never do work when we're ruined,' said she.

— 'You used to call home-life a hag-ridden dream,
And you'd sigh, and you'd sock; but at present
  you seem
headaches   To know not of megrims or melancho-ly!' —
'True. One's pretty lively when ruined,' said she.

— 'I wish I had feathers, a fine sweeping gown,
And a delicate face, and could strut about
  Town!' —
'My dear — a raw country girl, such as you be,
Cannot quite expect that. You ain't ruined,' said
  she.

THOMAS HARDY

To Lizbie Browne

I

Dear Lizbie Browne,
Where are you now?
In sun, in rain? —
Or is your brow
Past joy, past pain,
Dear Lizbie Browne?

II

Sweet Lizbie Browne,
How you could smile,
How you could sing! –
How archly wile
In glance-giving,
Sweet Lizbie Browne!

III

And, Lizbie Browne,
Who else had hair
Bay-red as yours,
Or flesh so fair
Bred out of doors,
Sweet Lizbie Browne?

IV

When, Lizbie Browne,
You had just begun
To be endeared
By stealth to one,
You disappeared
My Lizbie Browne!

V

Ay, Lizbie Browne,
So swift your life,
And mine so slow,
You were a wife
Ere I could show
Love, Lizbie Browne.

VI

Still, Lizbie Browne,
You won, they said,
The best of men
When you were wed . . .
Where went you then,
O Lizbie Browne?

VII

Dear Lizbie Browne,
I should have thought,
'Girls ripen fast,'
And coaxed and caught
You ere you passed,
Dear Lizbie Browne!

VIII

But, Lizbie Browne,
I let you slip;
Shaped not a sign;
Touched never your lip
With lip of mine,
Lost Lizbie Browne!

IX

So, Lizbie Browne,
When on a day
Men speak of me
As not, you'll say,
'And who was he?' –
Yes, Lizbie Browne!

THOMAS HARDY

Wha Fe Call I'

Miss Ivy, tell mi supmn,
An mi wan' yuh ansa good.
When yuh eat roun 12 o'clock,
Wassit yuh call yuh food?

For fram mi come yah mi confuse,
An mi noh know which is right,
Weddah dinnah a de food yuh eat midday,
Or de one yuh eat a night.

Mi know sey breakfus a de mawnin one
But cyan tell ef suppa a six or t'ree,
An one ting mi wi nebba undastan,
Is when yuh hab yuh tea.

Miss A dung a London ha lunch 12 o'clock,
An dinnah she hab bout t'ree,
Suppa she hab bout six o'clock,
But she noh hab noh tea.

Den mi go a Cambridge todda day,
Wi hab dinnah roun' bout two,
T'ree hour later mi frien she sey,
Mi hungry, how bout yuh?

Joe sey im tink a suppa time,
An mi sey yes, mi agree,
She halla, Suppa? a five o'clock,
Missis yuh mussa mean tea!

Den Sunday mi employer get up late,
Soh she noh hab breakfus nor lunch,
But mi hear she a talk bout 'Elevenses',
An one sinting dem call 'Brunch'.

Breakfus, elevenses, an brunch,
lunch, dinnah, suppa, tea,
Mi brain cyan wuk out which is which,
An when a de time fe hab i'.

For jus' when mi mek headway,
Sinting dreadful set mi back,
An dis when mi tink mi know dem all,
Mi hear bout one name snack.

bother

Mi noh tink mi a badda wid no name,
Mi dis a nyam when time mi hungry,
For doah mi 'tomach wi glad fe de food,
I' could care less whey mi call i'.

VALERIE BLOOM

De Souza Prabhu

No, I'm not going to
delve deep down and discover
I'm really de Souza Prabhu
even if Prabhu was no fool
and got the best of both worlds.
(Catholic Brahmin!
I can hear his chuckle still)

No matter that
my name is Greek
my surname Portuguese
my language alien.

There are ways
of belonging.

I belong with the lame ducks.

I heard it said
my parents wanted a boy.
I've done my best to qualify.
I hid the bloodstains
on my clothes
and let my breasts sag.
Words the weapon
to crucify.

EUNICE DE SOUZA

The Handsome Heart:

at a Gracious Answer

'But tell me, child, your choice; what shall I buy
You?' – 'Father, what you buy me I like best.'
With the sweetest air that said, still plied and
    pressed,
He swung to his first poised purport of reply.

What the heart is! which, like carriers let fly –
Doff darkness, homing nature knows the rest –
To its own fine function, wild and self-instressed,
Falls light as ten years long taught how to and
    why.

Mannerly-hearted! more than handsome face –
Beauty's bearing or muse of mounting vein,
All, in this case, bathed in high hallowing
    grace . . .

Of heaven what boon to buy you, boy, or gain
Not granted? – Only . . . O on that path you
    pace
Run all your race, O brace sterner that strain!

GERARD MANLEY HOPKINS

from Sweeney Agonistes

Well here again that don't apply
But I've gotta use words when I talk to you.
But here's what I was going to say.
He didn't know if he was alive
                    and the girl was dead
He didn't know if the girl was alive
                    and he was dead
He didn't know if they were both alive
                    or both were dead
If he was alive then the milkman wasn't
                    and the rent-collector wasn't
And if they were alive then he was dead.
There wasn't any joint
There wasn't any joint
For when you're alone
When you're alone like he was alone
You're either or neither
I tell you again it don't apply
Death or life or life or death
Death is life and life is death
I gotta use words when I talk to you
But if you understand or if you don't
That's nothing to me and nothing to you
We all gotta do what we gotta do
We're gona sit here and drink this booze
We're gona sit here and have a tune
We're gona stay and we're gona go
And somebody's gotta pay the rent

                    T. S. ELIOT

Joe Gargery's Epitaph on his Father

Whatsume'er the failings on his part,
Remember reader he were that good in his hart.

CHARLES DICKENS

from Ukulele Music

*Who would have thought it Sir, actually putting
  ME in a WRITING!
me and the Capting and ALL. What a turn up
  for the books.*

*Only, I must say I do not know HOW them
  people in poems
manage to say what they want – you know, in
  funny short lines,*

*or like what YOU do with them ones of yours
  sir, made of two lines like.
Still, when you're USED to it like, then you can
  speak natural.*

*Only, the newspaper man said that you was
  TRYING to sound like
low classes voices and that, only you wasn't no
  good –*

*you know, the CUTTING you left on yr desk
  top when I was waxing –
you know, that CRICKET which said you wasn't
  no good at all?*

when you got TERRIBLE, stamping and raging
    calling him stupid
and how the man was a FOOL, which was the
    day you took DRINK.

'What is to one class of minds and perceptions
    exaggeration,
is to another plain truth' (Dickens remarks in a
    brief

preface to *Chuzzlewit*). 'I have not touched one
    character straight from
life, but some counterpart of that very character
    has

asked me, incredulous, "Really now *did you* ever
    see, *really*,
anyone *really* like that?"' (this is the gist, not
    precise).

Well I can tell that old cricket that this is JUST
    how we speaks like,
me and the Capting and all (only not just in two
    lines).

PETER READING

Remains

for Robert Woof and Fleur Adcock

Though thousands traipse round Wordsworth's
   Lakeland shrine
imbibing bardic background, they don't see
nailed behind a shutter one lost line
with intimations of mortality
and immortality, but so discrete
it's never trespassed on 'the poet's' aura,
nor been scanned, as it is, five strong verse feet.

W. Martin's work needs its restorer,
and so from 1891 I use
the paperhanger's one known extant line
as the culture that I need to start off mine
and honour his one visit by the Muse,
then hide our combined labours underground
so once again it might be truly said
in words from Grasmere written by the dead:

our heads will be happen cold when this is
   found.

W. Martin
paperhanger
4 July 1891

TONY HARRISON

Index of Titles

Index of First Lines

Acknowledgements

For permission to reprint copyright material the publishers gratefully acknowledge the following:

Faber and Faber Limited and Random House, Inc. for 'The Cave of Making' by W. H. Auden from *W. H. Auden: Collected Poems* edited by Edward Mendelson (Faber, 1976) copyright © 1976 by Edward Mendelson, William Meredith and Monroe K. Spiers, Executors of the Estate of W. H. Auden; Louise Bennett for 'Independence' from *Jamaica labrish* (Sangster's Book Stores, Jamaica, 1983); New Beacon Books for 'Lucy's Letter' from *Lucy's Letters and Loving* by James Berry (New Beacon, 1982); Farrar, Straus & Giroux, Inc. for lines 'A washing hangs upon the line' from 'Songs for a Colored Singer', and for lines 'A new volcano has erupted' from 'Crusoe in England' by Elizabeth Bishop, from *Elizabeth Bishop: The Complete Poems 1927–1979* (Chatto & Windus, 1983/Farrar, Straus, Giroux, 1983) copyright © 1983 by Alice Helen Methfessel; Bogle-L'Ouverture Publications for 'Wha Fe Call I'' from *Touch Mi; Tell Mi!* by Valerie Bloom (Bogle L'Ouverture, 1983); Oxford University Press for 'Look wha' happen las' week at de O-', section I of 'Rites' from *The Arrivants* by Edward Kamau Brathwaite (OUP, 1973) © Edward Kamau Brathwaite 1973; The author and The Gallery Press, Loughcrew, Oldcastle, Co. Meath, Ireland, Bloodaxe Books Ltd and Wake Forest University Press for 'Hamlet' from *Belfast Confetti* by Ciaran Carson (Gallery Press and Wake Forest Press, 1989, and Bloodaxe Books, 1990); Curtis Brown Ltd, London, for 'The Lament of Swordy Well', 'The Badger', 'The Green Woodpecker's Nest' and 'Turkeys' by John Clare from *John Clare* (Oxford Authors), edited by Eric Robinson and David Powell (Oxford University Press, 1984), and for 'Pewits Nest' by John Clare from *Selected Poems and Prose of John Clare* edited by Eric Robinson and Geoffrey Summerfield (Oxford University Press, 1967) copyright © Eric Robinson 1967, 1984; Grafton Books, a division of The Collins Publishing Group, and Liveright Publishing Corporation for 'in Just-', section I of 'Chansons Innocentes' in 'Tulips and Chimneys (1923)' from *Complete Poems* Vol. I 1913–1935 by e. e. cummings (MacGibbon & Kee, 1968) copyright 1923, 1925, 1931, 1935 by e. e. cummings, © Marion Morehouse Cummings 1968; Eunice de Souza for 'De Souza Prabhu'; Little Brown and Company for 'Come Slowly Eden', 'Did the Harebell loose her girdle', 'I Have no life but this', 'I suppose the time will come', 'It's like the Light', 'Over the Fence', 'They Shut Me up in Prose', 'Under the Light yet Under' and 'The Wind Tapped like a Tired Man' from *The Complete Poems of Emily Dickinson* edited by Thomas H. Johnson (Cambridge, Mass: The Belknap Press, of Harvard University Press) copyright 1914, 1929, 1935, 1942 by Martha Dickinson Bianchi, copyright © renewed 1951, 1963 by Mary L. Hampson; Faber and Faber Limited for 'A Removal from Terry Street' from *Selected Poems 1964–1983* by Douglas Dunn (Faber, 1986); Faber and Faber Limited and Harcourt Brace Jovanovich, Inc. for 'Sweeney Raps' lines from 'Fragment of an Agon' from *Collected Poems 1909–1962* by T. S. Eliot (Faber, 1963) copyright 1936 by Harcourt Brace Jovanovich, Inc., copyright © 1964, 1963 by T. S. Eliot; Oxford University Press, Indian Branch, for 'The Patriot' by Nissim Ezekiel from *Very Indian Poems in Indian English*, I (OUP, Delhi); The Estate of Robert Frost and Henry Holt & Co. Inc. for 'Birches' by Robert Frost from *The Poetry of Robert Frost* edited by Edward Connery Lathem (Jonathan Cape, 1971/Holt, Rinehart &

Winston, 1969) copyright 1916, © 1969 by Holt, Rinehart and Winston, copyright 1944 by Robert Frost; Oxford University Press for 'First Time In' and 'Felling a Tree' by Ivor Gurney from *Collected Poems of Ivor Gurney* edited by P. J. Kavanagh (OUP, 1982) © Robin Haines, Sole Trustee of The Gurney Estate 1982; Bloodaxe Books Ltd for lines 'I've done my bit of mindless aggro too' from *v.* by Tony Harrison (Bloodaxe Books, 1985); The Peters, Fraser & Dunlop Group Ltd for 'Remains' from *Selected Poems* by Tony Harrison (Penguin, International Poets Series, 1989); Faber and Faber Limited and Farrar, Straus & Giroux Inc. for 'Broagh' from *Wintering Out* by Seamus Heaney (Faber, 1973) © 1972 by Seamus Heaney; Faber and Faber Limited and Harper Collins Publishers for 'Thistles' by Ted Hughes from *Ted Hughes: Selected Poems* (Faber, 1982/Harper & Row, 1972) copyright © 1961 by Ted Hughes; Mushinsha Ltd for 'Tired as I can be' by Bessie Jackson (Lucille Bogan) from *The Blues Line* edited by Eric Sackheim (Mushinsha, Tokyo, 1975); Polygon for 'De' from *Shoormal* by Robert Alan Jamieson (Polygon, 1986); R. L. C. Lorimer and the trustees of the W. L. Lorimer Memorial Trust Fund for two extracts of prose, 'In the beginning a aa things' from 'John's Gospel' Chapter I verses 1–18, and 'Peter Denies Christ' from 'Mark's Gospel' Chapter 14 verses 66–72, from *The New Testament in Scots* translated by William Laughton Lorimer (Southside (Publishers) Ltd, Edinburgh, 1983/Penguin 1985) copyright © 1983 R. L. C. Lorimer; Mushinsha Ltd for 'Brown Skin Girl' by Tommy McClennan from *The Blues Line* edited by Eric Sackheim (Mushinsha, Tokyo, 1975); Macmillan Publishing Co, New York, for 'The Bonnie Broukit Bairn', 'Farmer's Death', 'Sunny Gale', 'The Watergaw' and 'Whip-the-World' by Hugh MacDiarmid from *The Complete Poems of Hugh MacDiarmid* Vol. I edited by Michael Grieve and W. R. Aitken (Martin Brian & O'Keefe, 1978/Penguin, 1985) © copyright 1978 Christopher Murray Grieve; Faber and Faber Limited for 'Prayer before Birth' and 'Death of an old Lady' by Louis MacNeice from *The Collected Poems of Louis MacNeice* edited by E. R. Dodds (Faber, 1966); Random Century Ltd for 'Ower t'Ills o Bingley', lines from 'The Ballad of the Yorkshire Ripper' from *The Ballad of the Yorkshire Ripper and other poems* by Blake Morrison (Chatto & Windus, 1987); Faber and Faber Limited and Wake Forest University Press for 'Quoof' from *Quoof* by Paul Muldoon (Faber, 1983/Wake Forest, 1983); Angus & Robertson (UK) for 'The Greenhouse Vanity' from *Dog Fox Field* by Les Murray (Collins/Angus & Robertson, Australia 1990); 'The Ghost' is reprinted from *O'Brien's Lusorium* (1782) in *The New Oxford Book of Eighteenth-Century Poetry* edited by Roger Lonsdale (OUP, 1984); Opal Palmer for 'Wasting Time'; Peter Reading for 'Who Would Have Thought it Sir, actually putting ME in a WRITING!' from *Ukelele Music* (Secker & Warburg, 1985); Christopher Reid for 'firs', lines from 'Memres of Alfred Stoker'; Mrs Shuyler Jackson for 'The Wind, the Clock, the We' by Laura Riding from *Selected Poems: In Five Sets* (Faber, 1970); The Trustees of the National Library of Scotland for 'Summer is By' and 'The Three Puddocks' by William Soutar from *Poems of William Soutar: A New Selection* edited by W. R. Aitken (Scottish Academic Press, 1988); Oxford University Press for 'Utah' from *Selected Poems 1956–1986* by Anne Stevenson (OUP, 1987) © Anne Stevenson 1987; Faber and Faber Limited and Farrar, Straus & Giroux, Inc. for 'Pomme Arac' section 2 of *Sainte Lucie* by Derek Walcott from *Collected Poems* (Faber, 1986); The Keeper of Western Manuscripts, The Bodleian Library, Oxford, for 'What makes me write', lines from 'A Poem made by [a Friend of] mine in Answere to One who Askt w[hy s]he wrotte', by Hester Wyat (Bod. MS Rawl. D. 360, fol. 53) quoted in Introduction by Germaine Greer to *Kissing the Rod* edited by Germaine Greer, Susan Hastings, Jeslyn Medoff, Melinda Sansone (Virago, 1988).

Faber and Faber Limited apologize for any errors or omissions in the above list and would be grateful to be notified of any corrections that should be incorporated in the next edition or reprint of this volume.

UXBRIDGE COLLEGE LIBRARY